STITCH
step by step

P9-BIT-280

STITCH
step by step

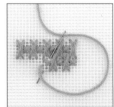

Maggi Gordon and Ellie Vance

LONDON, NEW YORK, MUNICH,
MELBOURNE, DELHI

US Editors Margaret Parrish and Shannon Beatty

DK INDIA
Senior Editor Chitra Subramanyam
Assistant Editor Ekta Sharma
Assistant Art Editors Era Chawla, Divya PR
Managing Editor Glenda Fernandes
Managing Art Editor Navidita Thapa
Production Manager Pankaj Sharma
DTP Manager Sunil Sharma
Senior DTP Designer Dheeraj Arora
DTP Operator Anurag Trivedi

DK UK
Project Editors Cressida Tuson, Shashwati Tia Sarkar
Project Art Editors Jane Ewart, Glenda Fisher
Design Assistant Danaya Bunnag
Managing Editor Dawn Henderson
Managing Art Editor Christine Keilty
Senior Jacket Creative Nicola Powling
Production Editor Maria Elia
Senior Production Controller Alice Sykes
Creative Technical Support Sonia Charbonnier

Material first published in the United States in *The Needlecraft Book*, 2010
This edition first published in 2011 by DK Publishing
375 Hudson Street, New York, New York 10014

11 12 13 10 9 8 7 5 4 3 2 1
001—179847—Aug/2011

Copyright © 2011 Dorling Kindersley Limited.
All rights reserved.

Without limiting the rights under copyright reserved above, no part of this
publication may be reproduced, stored in or introduced to a retrieval system, or
transmitted, in any form, or by any means (electronic, mechanical, photocopying,
recording or otherwise), without the prior permission of both the copyright owner
and the above publisher of this book.

Published in Great Britain by Dorling Kindersley Limited.

A catalog record for this book is available from the Library of Congress.

ISBN 978-0-7566-8225-5
DK books are available at special discounts when purchased in bulk for sales
promotions, premiums, fund-raising, or educational use. For details, contact: DK
Publishing Special Markets, 375 Hudson Street, New York, New York 10014 or
SpecialSales@dk.com.

Color reproduction by Media Development & Printing Ltd.
Printed and bound in Singapore by Tien Wah Press.

Discover more at **www.dk.com**

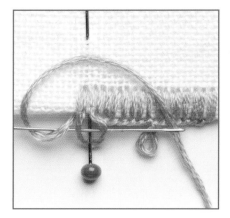

CONTENTS

INTRODUCTION

If you want to master the art of embroidery, a type of needlework that has been used for millennia to decorate, enhance, embellish, and even repair textiles, *Stitch Step By Step* will help you learn the skills required. Materials range from simple yarn to gold and silver thread worked on the finest silk or the coarsest sacking, and the stitching itself can be soothing and therapeutic, as well as providing useful and beautiful items to wear and decorate a home.

The book covers the main types of embroidery, beginning with a Gallery showing examples of every stitch detailed in the book. It explains the basic techniques for Surface Embroidery, the most widely practiced form; Openwork, in which threads are either separated or removed from the fabric altogether to create delicate, lacelike effects; Smocking; Beadwork; and Needlepoint, which is also known as Canvaswork because it is worked on canvas. Information for starting and finishing, as well as instructions for working each stitch, are all detailed in clear, easy-to-follow, step-by-step photographs.

I hope it will provide inspiration and be a valuable reference tool, and that you, too, can experience the pleasure that I find in stitching.

Maggi Gordon

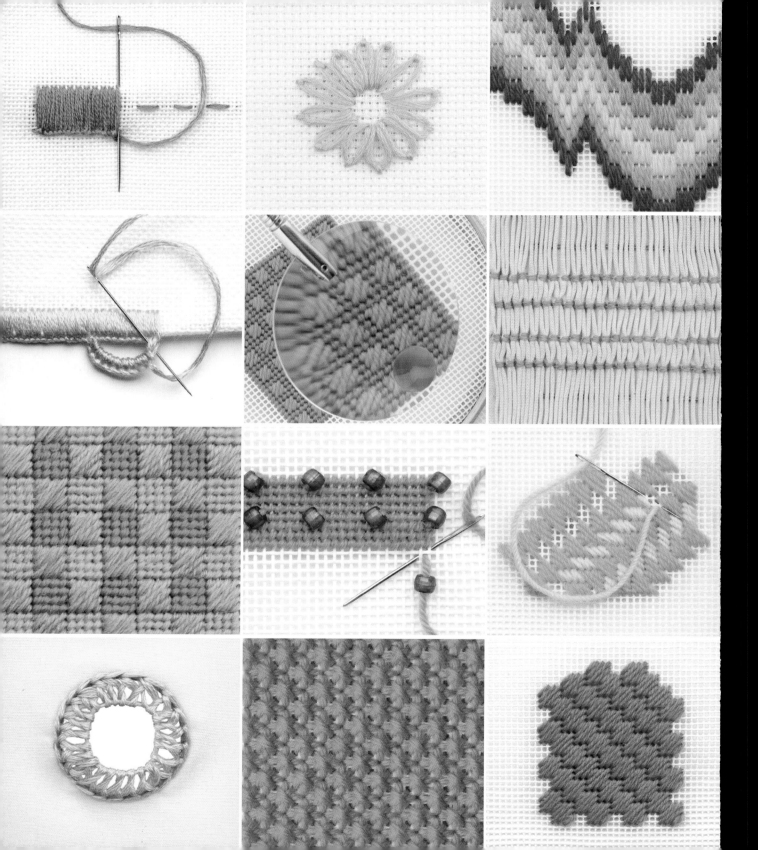

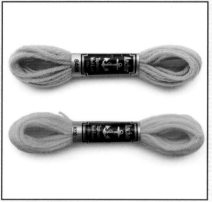

TOOLS AND MATERIALS

Tools and materials

The basic tools and materials that are essential for embroidery are simple and easy to obtain, although there are a few more elaborate frames that are useful for certain advanced techniques, and some fabrics and threads that are available only through specialty suppliers. Many products can now be found via the Internet.

Basic sewing kit

A well-equipped sewing kit will include all of the items shown below and many more, depending on the type of stitching that you do regularly. It is important that a suitable container is used to keep your tools together, so that they will be readily on hand, and to keep them organized.

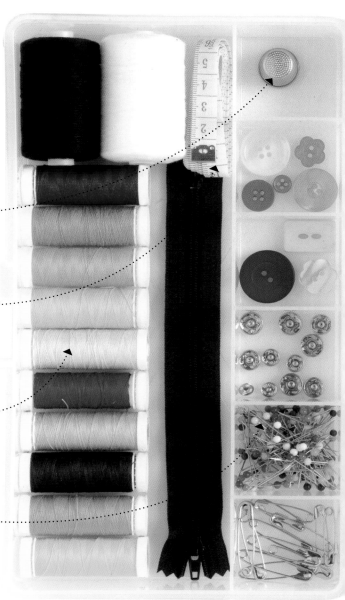

Thimble

This is useful to protect the end of your finger when stitching. Thimbles are available in various shapes and sizes. See page 24.

Tape measure

Essential, to help measure fabric, seams, etc. Choose one that gives both inches and centimeters. A tape measure made of plastic is best as it will not stretch. See page 22.

Threads

A selection of threads and yarns for embroidery and needlepoint in a variety of colors. Some threads are made of cotton or silk while others are wool or synthetics. See page 20.

Pins

Needed to hold the fabric together prior to sewing and finishing your work. There are different types of pins for different types of work.

Embroidery scissors
Small pair of scissors with very sharp points, to clip threads close to the fabric. See page 22.

Needles
A good selection of different types of needles for sewing by hand. This will enable you to tackle any stitching project. See page 14.

Seam ripper
To remove any stitches that have been made in the wrong place. Various sizes of seam rippers are available. Keep the cover on when not in use to protect the sharp point. See page 24.

Pin cushion
To keep your needles and pins safe and clean. Choose one that has a fabric cover and is firm. See page 24.

Cutting shears
Required for cutting fabric or canvas. When buying, select a pair that feels comfortable in your hand and that is not too heavy.

Sewing gauge
A handy gadget for small measurements. The slide can be set to measure hem depths, buttonhole diameters, and much more.

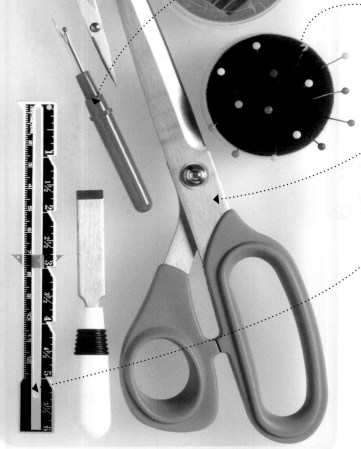

Needles

There are several types of needle suitable for embroidery, each used for a specific purpose. All come in different thicknesses and lengths. Select one that can pass smoothly through the fabric; the eye of the needle should be large enough to take the required thread easily.

Crewel needle
Crewel needles have sharp points and an eye designed to take thicker-than-normal thread and are ideal for most surface embroidery on plain-weave fabrics.

Tapestry needle
Blunt-ended tapestry needles should always be used on even-weaves to avoid splitting the threads of the fabric. These needles have large eyes to accommodate relatively thick threads and come in sizes ranging from 26 (the smallest) to 13 (the largest).

Chenille needle
Chenilles are sharp-pointed and heavier, and take thicker threads for work on heavy-weight fabrics.

Beading needle
Beading needles are long and very fine, so that they can pass easily through tiny bead holes.

Fabrics

There are plenty of fabrics, particularly even-weaves, especially for embroidery, but almost any plain-weave fabric, from fine silk to cotton twill, can be used as a background. Even-weaves are linen or cotton woven in a regular square grid. Single- and double-thread even-weaves are available in a variety of sizes, which are referred to as thread counts. The more threads there are per inch, the finer the fabric. Plain-weaves are ideal for freestyle embroidery.

EVEN-WEAVE FABRICS

Aida double thread
Double thread even-weave fabrics are stiff and widely used for cross-stitch and other counted-stitch techniques. Aida is easy to use as the threads are clear and easy to count.

Binca double thread
Similar to Aida, Binca even-weave fabrics are available in many colors and textures.

OTHER EVEN-WEAVES
Single thread
Single-thread cottons and linens are used mainly for drawn-thread and pulled-fabric techniques.

14   Tools and materials

PLAIN-WEAVE FABRICS

Cotton
Easy to work and economical, cotton fabrics are a good choice for general embroidery where you do not need to count the threads in order to space the stitches evenly.

Silk
A classic choice for embroidered projects, silk is the perfect base for working in silk threads.

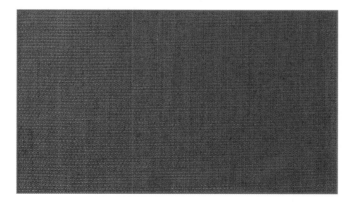

Linen
With a heavier, open weave, linen is easy to work and provides a stable base for embroidered designs.

Types of canvas

Needlepoint is worked on a fabric known as canvas (hence, the alternative name "canvaswork"). This has an open-mesh construction: strong threads, usually of cotton, are woven with spaces in between and the stitches are worked over one or more of these threads. The number of threads per 1in (2.5cm) is called the count, gauge, or mesh. Needlepoint canvas comes in several colors—tan, white, cream, and yellow—and also in paper or plastic versions.

Interlock canvas

This is a special type of single-thread canvas in which each lengthwise, or warp, thread actually consists of two threads twisted around the crosswise, weft, threads. The result is a more stable construction—less likely to become distorted. Unlike ordinary single canvas, interlock can be used for half-cross stitch (see page 162).

Single, or mono, canvas

This is constructed of single threads crossing each other in a simple over-and-under weave. It comes in a wide range of gauges and is suitable for nearly all stitches. Its only drawback is that some stitches—or a tight tension—can pull it out of shape; however, a little distortion can be corrected in the blocking process (see page 192).

Rug canvas

Available in 3-, 5-, and 7-count, this has two paired threads in each direction, which can be in an open, penelope-type weave or joined in an interlock-type weave. Some rug canvas has contrasting threads marking out 10-hole squares. This canvas is often used for wall hangings and large pillows, as well as rugs.

Double, or penelope, canvas

In this type of canvas both warp and weft are formed of pairs of threads. This, too, is a relatively strong construction. The gauge is often expressed as the number of holes, sometimes with the thread count given afterward. For example, a 10/20 penelope canvas has 10 pairs of threads per 1in (2.5cm). Stitches are normally worked over the paired threads, treating them as one, but the threads can be separated and worked over singly to produce areas of fine stitching if desired.

Perforated paper

Available in several colors, this 14-count material is especially suitable for greeting cards.

Hoops and frames

Hoops and frames are used to hold the ground fabric taut, which keeps the grain of the fabric straight and the stitches regular. Hoops consist of two thin rings; the fabric is placed between them. Frames are straight-sided. Both can be attached to floor and table stands that allow you to keep both hands free for stitching.

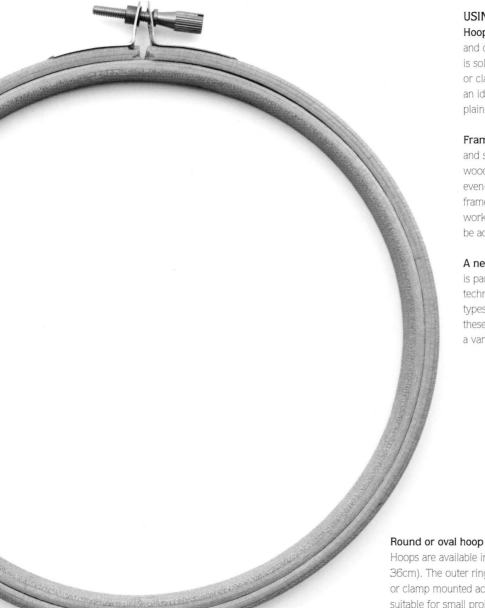

USING HOOPS AND FRAMES

Hoops are made of wood or plastic, and can be round or oval. The inner ring is solid, while the outer one has a screw or clamp that can be adjusted to achieve an ideal tautness. They are best used with plain-weave fabrics and fine even-weaves.

Frames, called scroll or slate frames and stretchers, are traditionally made of wood. They are used mainly for mounting even-weaves and needlepoint canvas. Scroll frames are adjustable (see opposite), while work in stretcher frames, whose size cannot be adjusted, should fit inside the frame.

A new type of frame of plastic tubing is particularly useful for many beading techniques, but can also be used for most types of embroidery. Called Q-Snaps, these straight-sided frames come in a variety of sizes.

Round or oval hoop
Hoops are available in various sizes, from 5 to 14in (12.5 to 36cm). The outer ring is adjusted with a small tension screw or clamp mounted across a split in the ring. They are most suitable for small projects.

FRAME CHOICE

The use of a frame is optional. The main advantages of using one are that it helps to prevent the canvas from distorting and assists you in maintaining an even stitch tension. Only rectangular frames are suitable for needlepoint; canvas is too stiff for a hoop frame and would become distorted if forced into one.

An upholstered frame: This is less widely available but provides a pleasant way to work. You simply pin the canvas to the padding and move it around if necessary. A matching sandbag will hold the frame balanced on the edge of a table for two-handed stitching.

Artist's stretcher frame: This consists of two pairs of wooden (painter's) canvas stretchers, which slot into each other at the corners. They are available at art-supply stores. Make sure that the inner edges of the frame will be larger than the stitching area of the needlepoint.

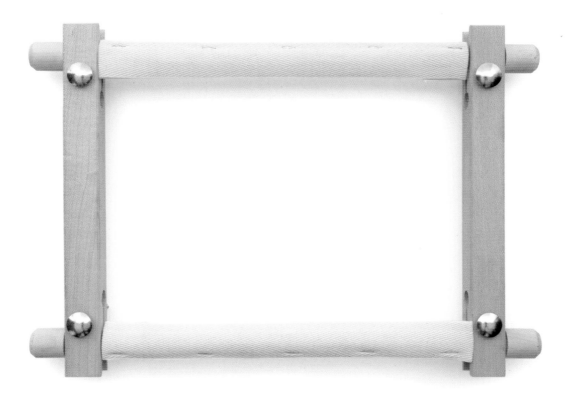

Square frame

Also known as a roller frame or adjustable frame, this is specially designed for embroidery, including needlepoint, and consists of two wooden rollers and two side slats. Some models are designed to stand on the floor or on a table, leaving both hands free for stitching. Lengths of webbing stapled to the bars hold the work, which can be rolled up as required to expose new areas.

Threads and yarns

Embroidery threads can be thick or thin. They are made from cotton, silk, wool, and linen as well as synthetics. Some threads are single ply, while others are spun in multiples and can be divided into single strands: the fewer the filaments, the finer the embroidered line. The most popular threads for needlepoint are made of wool. There are three types of wool yarn suitable for this work: crewel, Persian, and tapestry. Other kinds of thread, such as stranded cotton and silk floss, pearl cotton, and metallic threads are also used.

SILK THREADS

Stranded silk
Silk has a soft quality, and stranded threads can be divided to produce very fine threads.

Twisted silk
Twisted silk has a beautiful sheen and works well on fine-count canvas.

Silk buttonhole
This is a strong thread that is similar in thickness to pearl cotton.

Rayon silk
This is a slightly cheaper option, but is very soft and has a rich sheen.

COTTON THREADS

Stranded floss
This is a loosely twisted 6-strand thread that can easily be divided into single threads.

Pearl cotton
This is a strong, twisted thread that cannot be divided. It has a smooth sheen and keeps its shape well without kinking.

OTHER SPECIAL COTTON THREADS

Flower thread: This is a fine, single-ply cotton thread. It has a matte finish and is good for cross stitch.

Soft embroidery thread: A soft, matte thread that is easy to work and suitable for half-cross stitch and long stitch. It is often used in needlepoint.

Coton a broder: A pure cotton thread that is tightly twisted with a lovely luster. It is commonly used for whitework.

YARN

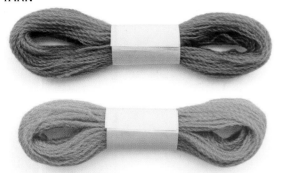

Crewel yarn
This is a fine 2-ply yarn that can be used in any multiple of strands to suit the gauge of the canvas. Individual strands blend together smoothly, producing a soft texture.

OTHER WOOL YARNS
Persian yarn
Thicker than crewel yarn, this comes in a triple strand, of which the individual strands can easily be separated. You can use one or more strands in the needle.

Tapestry yarn
This comes in a smooth, uniform 4-ply strand, which is normally used singly, on 10- to 14-count canvas.

OTHER THREADS AND BEADS

Beads
Beads add texture to a needlepoint project. They can be used for beaded tent stitch (see page 164) or simply sewn to the finished surface.

Metallic thread
Combine metallic threads with a more conventional wool or cotton yarn in the needle to keep them from kinking.

Knitting yarn
It is possible to use knitting yarn in a needlepoint project but some soft yarns may fray and those that stretch may cause tension problems.

Silk thread
A glossy, silk thread will add some sheen or highlights to stitches but use with care as it may snag.

General equipment

Almost all the equipment you need for stitching can be found in a well-stocked sewing basket: large and small sharp scissors for cutting fabrics and threads, marking pens and pencils, and measuring equipment. Add a thimble if you use one, and perhaps a pin cushion, and you are ready to start. For needlepoint, tapestry needles, scissors, and tape to bind the canvas are the bare essentials. However, you will need some other tools and materials for finishing a project, for creating your own designs, and simply for convenience.

CUTTING TOOLS

Small embroidery scissors
Essential for cutting threads. Ensure that they are sharp in order to cut neat ends.

Bent-handled fabric scissors
Use large, sharp scissors for cutting your fabric or canvas to size.

Scissors
Keep a separate pair of scissors dedicated to cutting paper, to avoid blunting the blade of dressmaker's scissors used for cutting canvas or fabric.

MEASURING TOOLS

Set square
Useful for drawing right angles when reshaping needlepoint.

Tape measure and ruler
Measuring equipment is useful to have close at hand, for checking the size of your work and thread counts.

MARKING AIDS

Tracing paper
This is ideal for converting designs. Gridded tracing paper is ideal for translating designs to chart form.

Dressmaker's carbon paper
This is ideal for transferring your embroidery design to the fabric ground.

Graph paper
This is used for tracing motifs and complete needlepoint designs. Gridded tracing paper is ideal for converting designs to chart form.

Colored paper
Use colored paper to cut out shapes when designing motifs.

Drawing paper
Keep a sketch pad on hand for copying needlepoint designs or sketching ideas.

Colored pencils
Keep a selection in a wide range of colors for making charts or sketching designs.

Permanent fabric marker
This is useful for transferring or tracing the needlepoint design outline onto the canvas.

Pencil
Essential for sketching and tracing designs.

Felt-tip pen
This is useful for darkening outlines on motifs before tracing or transferring.

Useful extras

Seam ripper
For unpicking seams or correcting mistakes.

Tweezers
These are very useful for pulling out mistakes.

Thimble
A thimble will prevent you from accidently pricking your finger as you work and staining your embroidery.

Artist's paintbrush
Choose a suitably sized brush for applying paints to canvas.

Pin cushion
A useful item to have by your side when finishing or sewing your embroidery.

Acrylic paints (permanent)
These are specially made for crafts; they are easy to brush or sponge onto canvas and can be mixed to produce desired shades.

Masking tape
Used for binding the edges of the canvas to protect it while you work.

Woven tape
This is used, along with string, for attaching the canvas to a scroll frame.

Tags
Use these for labeling yarns with shade numbers.

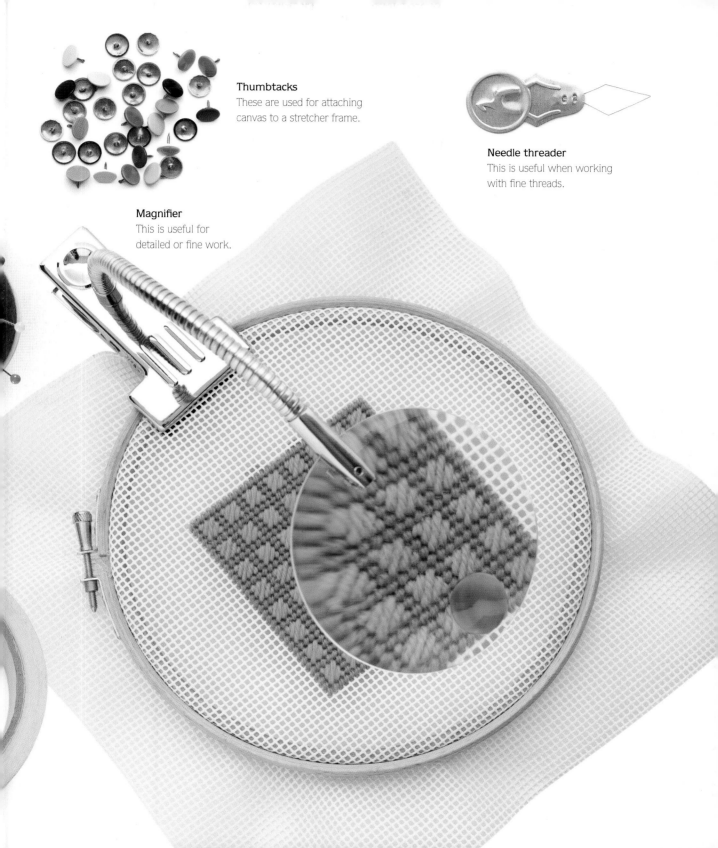

Thumbtacks
These are used for attaching canvas to a stretcher frame.

Needle threader
This is useful when working with fine threads.

Magnifier
This is useful for detailed or fine work.

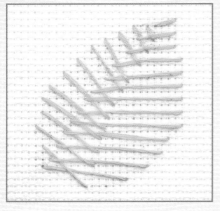 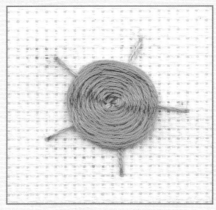 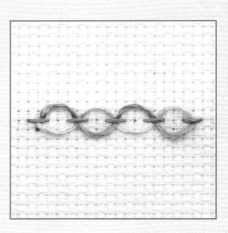

STITCH GALLERY

Stitch Gallery

These pages provide a quick visual reference for all the stitches in this chapter. Each stitch is shown as a final sample to allow you to find the appropriate stitch quickly. The stitches are grouped according to type to show all the possibilities and alternatives at a glance.

Surface embroidery

CROSS STITCH

Double-sided stitch (p65)

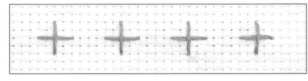

St. George cross stitch (p67)

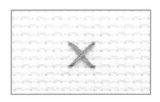

Individual cross stitch (p64)

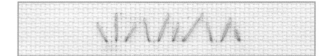

Serial cross stitch (p65)

Long-armed cross stitch (p66)

FLAT STITCHES

Straight stitch (p67)

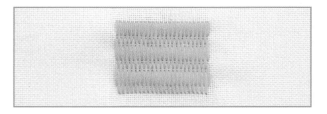

Long and short stitch (p68)

Leaf stitch (p69)

Fern stitch (p70)

OUTLINE STITCHES

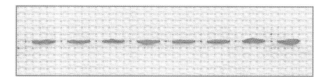

Running stitch (p71)

Backstitch (p72)

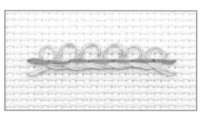

Stem stitch (p72)

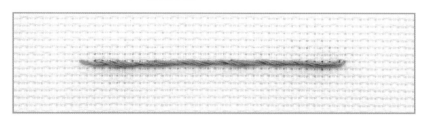

Whipped backstitch (p73)

Pekinese stitch (p73)

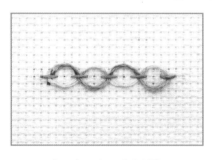

Laced running stitch (p71)

Holbein stitch (p73)

Split stitch (p74)

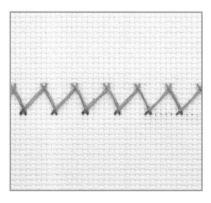

Herringbone stitch (p74)

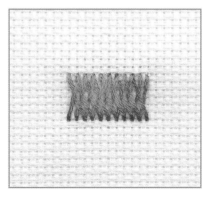

Closed herringbone stitch (p75)

Chevron stitch (p75)

FILLING STITCH

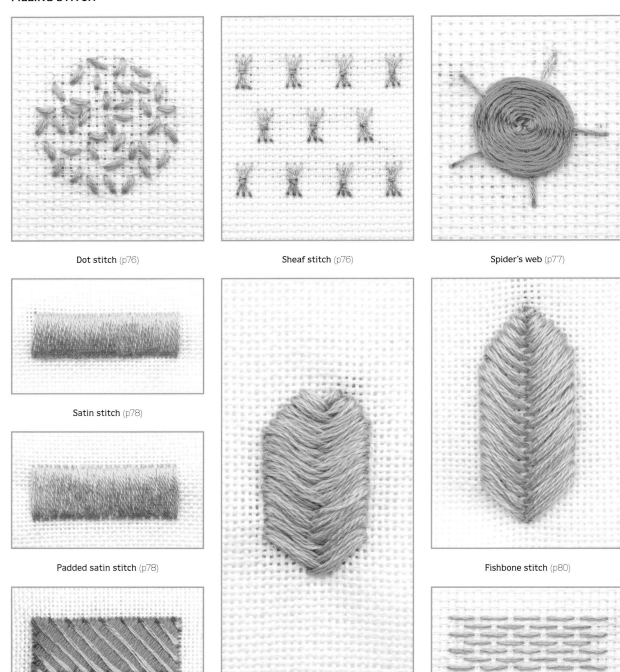

Dot stitch (p76)

Sheaf stitch (p76)

Spider's web (p77)

Satin stitch (p78)

Padded satin stitch (p78)

Whipped satin stitch (p79)

Flat stitch (p79)

Fishbone stitch (p80)

Darning stitch (p80)

Stitch gallery

LOOPED STITCHES

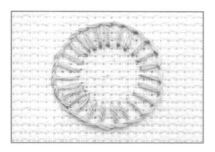 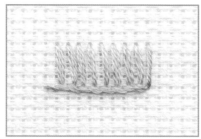 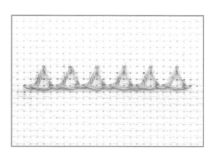

Blanket and buttonhole stitch (p81)   Closed buttonhole stitch (p82)

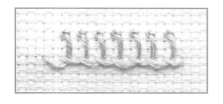 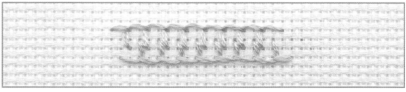

Knotted buttonhole stitch (p82)   Double buttonhole stitch (p83)

 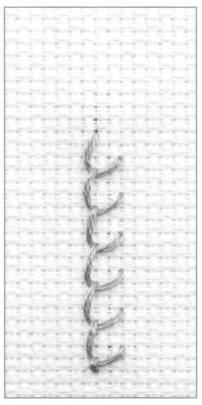 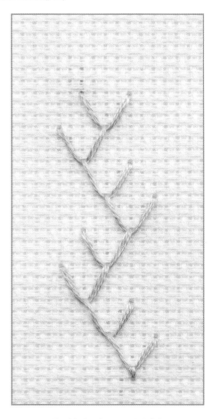

Feather stitch (p83)   Single feather stitch (p84)   Double feather stitch (p84)

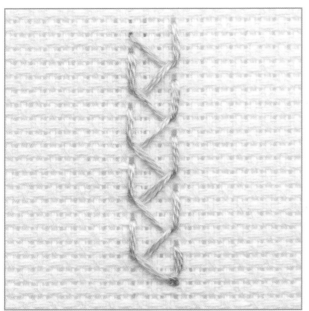

Closed feather stitch (p85)

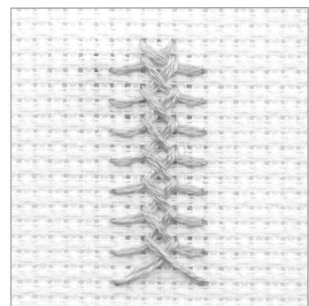

Vandyke stitch (p86)

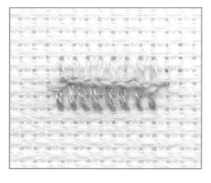

Loop stitch (p85)

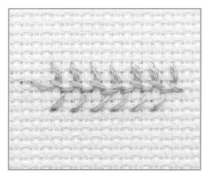

Cretan stitch (p87)

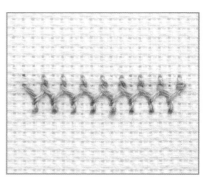

Open Cretan stitch (p87)

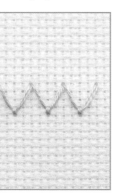

Fly stitch (p88)

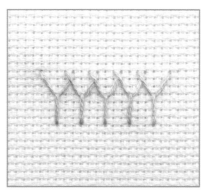

Braided fly stitch (p88)

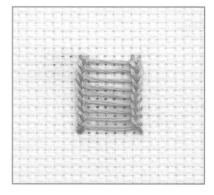

Ladder stitch (p89)

32 Stitch gallery

CHAINED STITCHES

Daisy stitch (p90)

Chain stitch (p90)

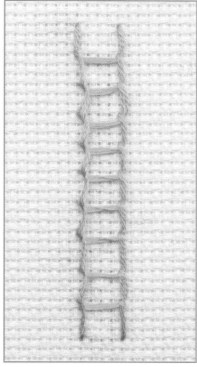

Open chain stitch (p91)

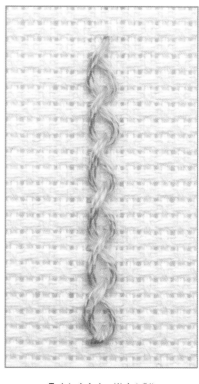

Twisted chain stitch (p91)

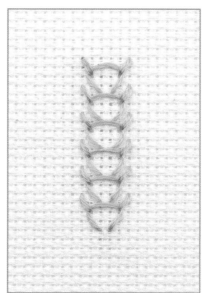

Feathered chain stitch (p92)

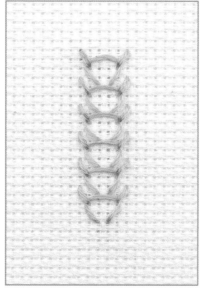

Wheatear stitch (p93)

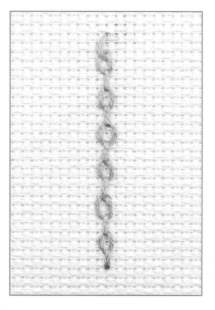

Cable chain stitch (p94)

Stitch gallery   **33**

KNOTTED STITCHES

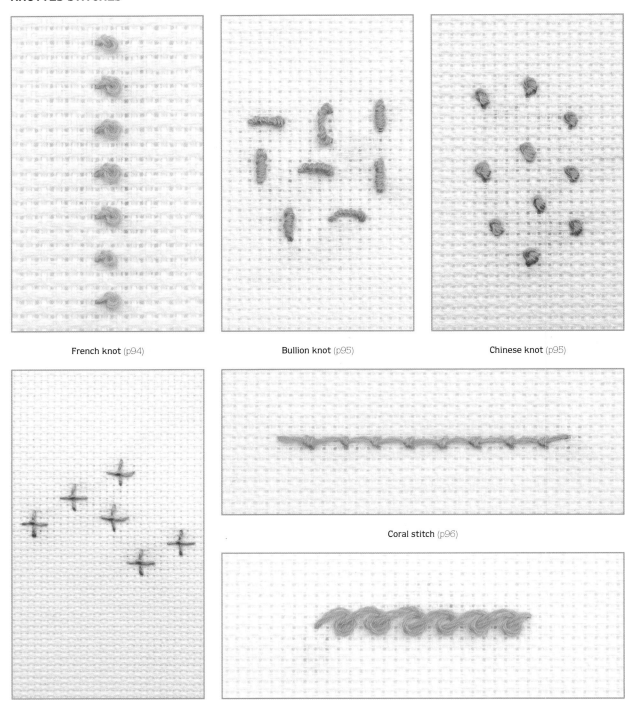

French knot (p94)

Bullion knot (p95)

Chinese knot (p95)

Four-legged knot (p96)

Coral stitch (p96)

Scroll stitch (p97)

Stitch gallery

COUCHING

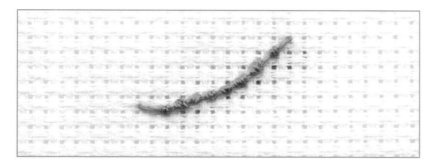

Couching stitch (p96)

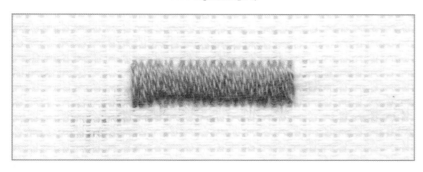

Overcast trailing (p98)

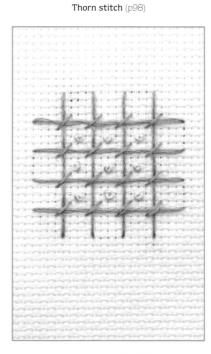

Thorn stitch (p98)

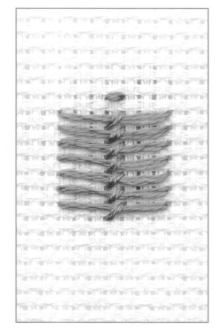

Roumanian stitch (p99)

Bokhara stitch (p100)

Jacobean trellis (p101)

Openwork

WHITEWORK

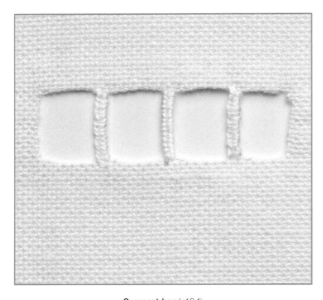

Overcast bar (p104)

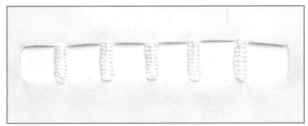

Buttonhole bar (p105)

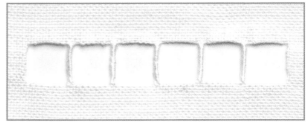

Woven bar (p105)

Looped edging (p106)

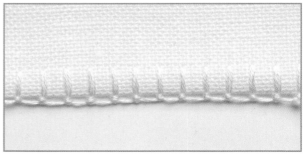

Antwerp edging (p106)

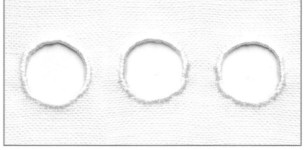

Overcast eyelets (p107)

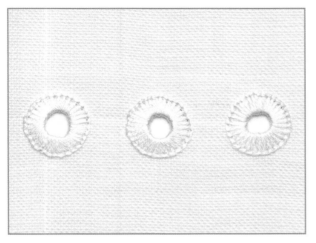

Buttonhole eyelet (p107)

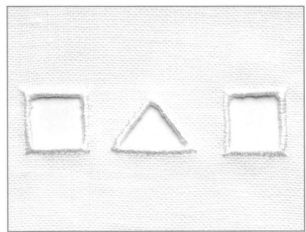

Square eyelet (p108)

Solid edges (p108)

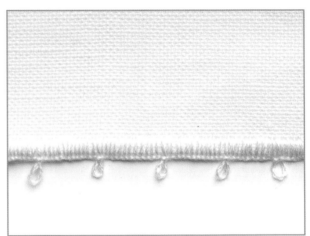

Loop picot (p109)

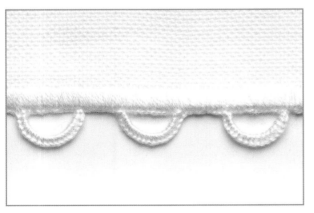

Ring picot (p109)

Eyelet edges (p110)

PULLED THREAD WORK

Four-sided stitch (p110)

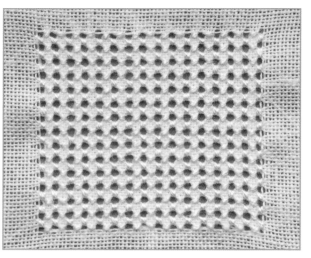

Punch stitch (p111)

Chessboard filling (p113)

Window stitch (p113)

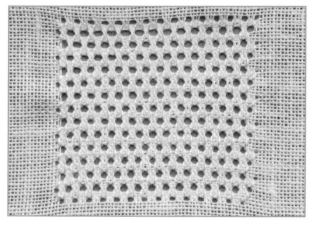

Wave stitch (p115)

Mosaic filling (p114)

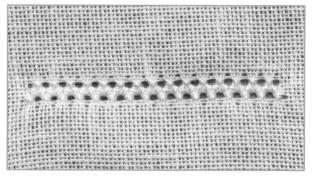

Three-sided stitch (p116)

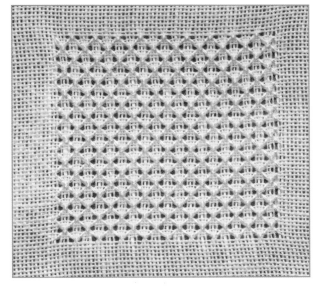

Honeycomb filling stitch (p112)

Step stitch (p112)

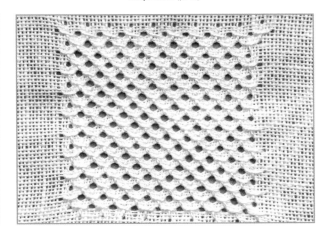

Coil filling (p116)

Diagonal raised band (p117)

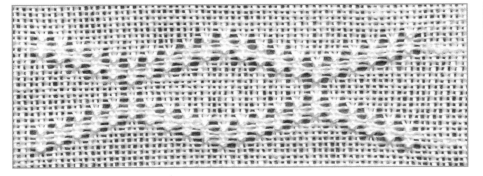

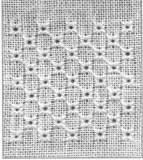

Diamond filling (p117)

Algerian eye (p118)

DRAWN THREAD WORK

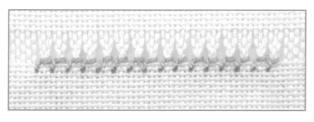

Hemstitch (p119)

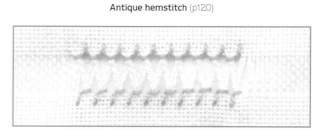

Antique hemstitch (p120)

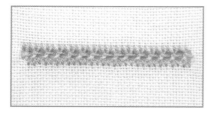

Ladder hemstitch (p120)

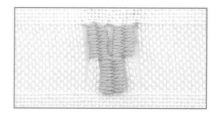

Zigzag hemstitch (p120)

Interlaced hemstitch (p121)

Diamond hemstitch (p122)

Woven hemstitch (p123)

INSERTIONS

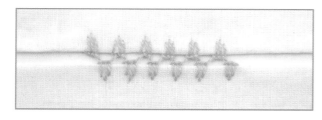

Buttonhole insertion stitch (p124)

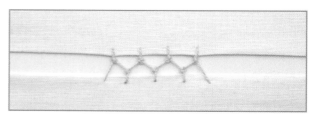

Knotted insertion stitch (p124)

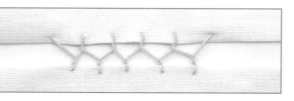

Twisted insertion stitch (p125)

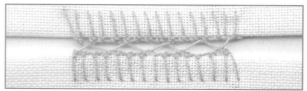

Laced insertion stitch (p125)

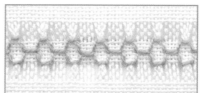

Smocking

SMOCKING BASICS

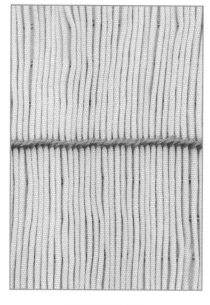

Rope stitch (p129)

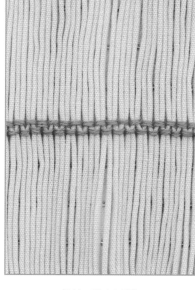

Cable stitch (p129)

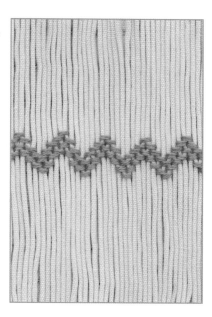

Vandyke stitch (p129)

HONEYCOMB SMOCKING

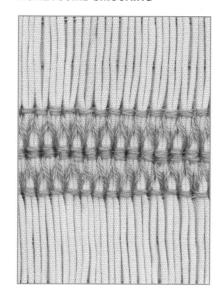

Closed honeycomb stitch (p130)

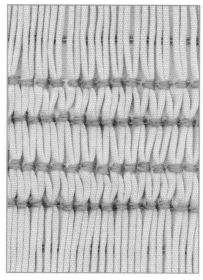

Open honeycomb stitch (p130)

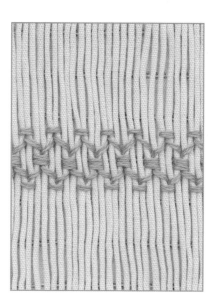

Honeycomb chevron stitch (p131)

Beadwork

BEADS

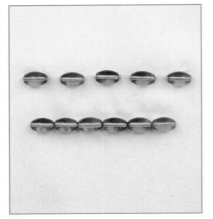

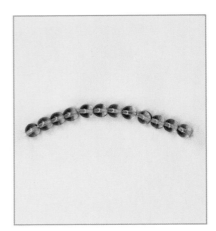

Single bead (p134)

Couching (p134)

Spot stitch (p135)

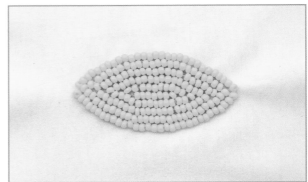

Lazy squaw filling (p135)

Ojibwa filling (p136)

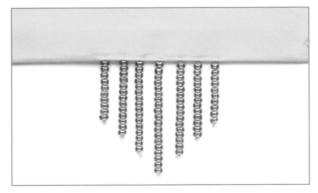

Beaded fringe (p136)

Loop fringe (p137)

SEQUINS

Single sequin (p137)

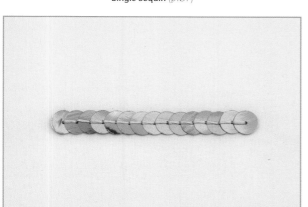

Sequin chain (p138)

Beaded sequin (p138)

MIRRORWORK

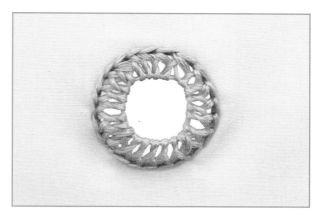

Single thread method (p139)

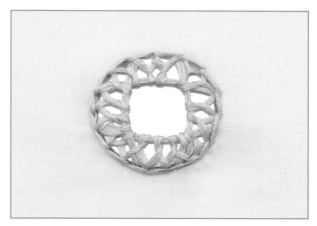

Double thread method (p141)

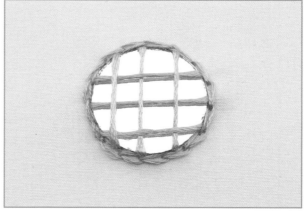

Lattice (p141)

Needlepoint

Use this gallery to find the best stitches for your needlepoint projects. The stitches are grouped according to type to show all the possibilities and alternatives at a glance, whether you are looking for a simple textured stitch or trying something more complicated.

DIAGONAL STITCHES

Continental tent stitch (p160)

Basketweave (p161)

Beaded tent stitch (p164)

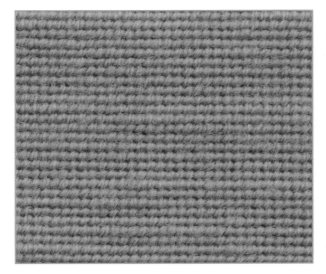

Half-cross stitch (p162)

Tramé (p163)

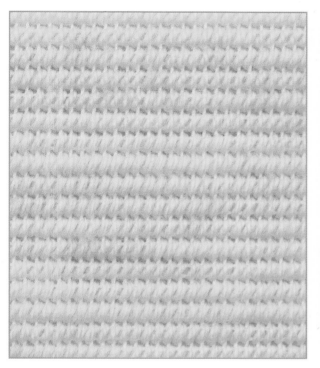

Slanted gobelin stitch (p164)

Cushion stitch (p166)

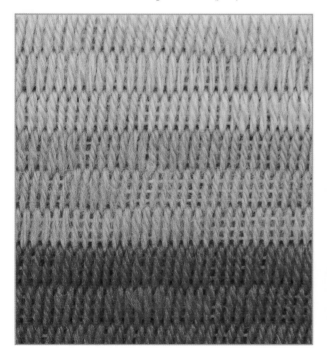

Encroaching gobelin stitch (p165)

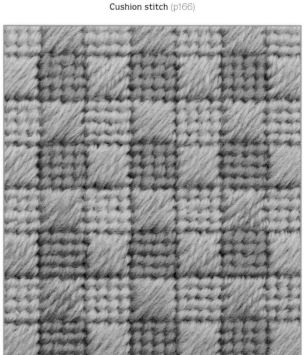

Checker stitch (p167)

Stitch gallery 45

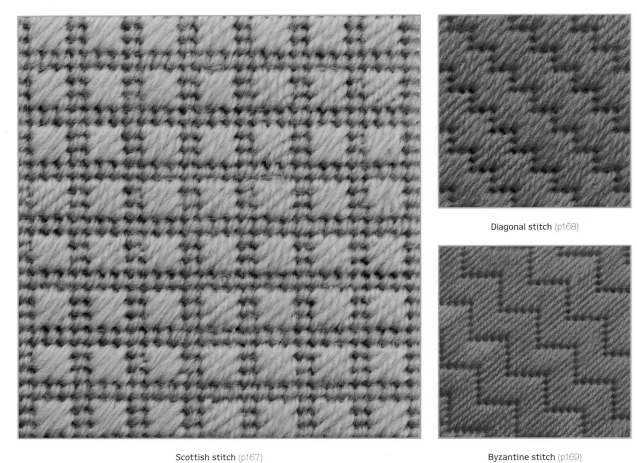

Diagonal stitch (p168)

Byzantine stitch (p169)

Scottish stitch (p167)

Moorish stitch (p169)

Mosaic stitch: checkerboard effect (p168)

Stitch gallery

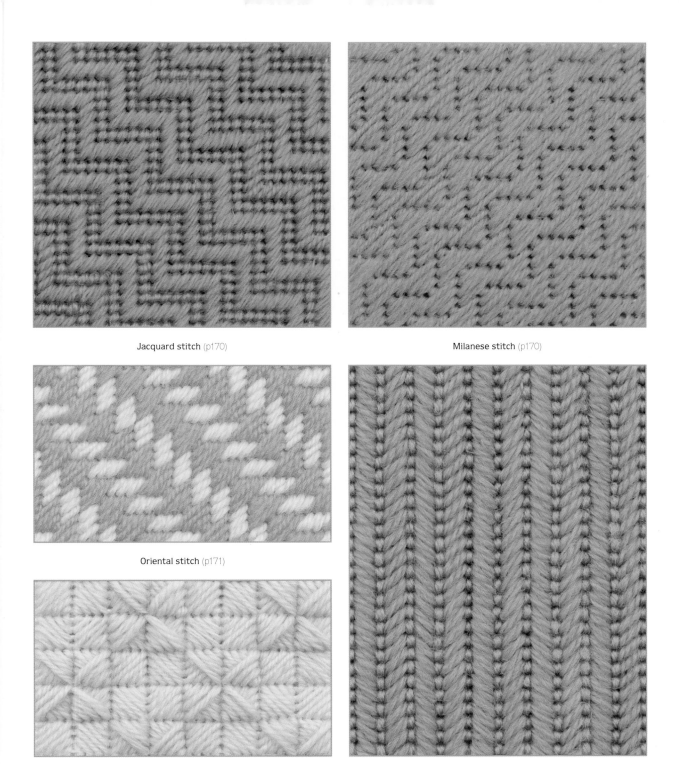

Jacquard stitch (p170)

Milanese stitch (p170)

Oriental stitch (p171)

Crossed corners cushion stitch (p172)

Stem stitch (p171)

Stitch gallery   47

STRAIGHT STITCHES

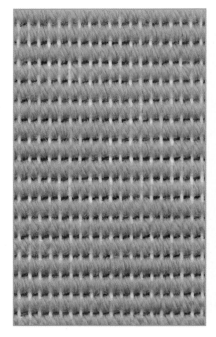

Straight gobelin stitch (p173)

Interlocking straight stitch (p174)

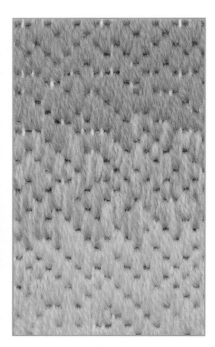

Random straight stitch (p175)

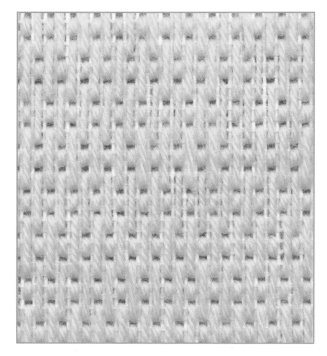

Parisian stitch (p175)

Double twill stitch (p176)

Twill stitch (p176)

Weaving stitch (p178)

Hungarian stitch (p178)

Pavilion diamond stitch (p177)

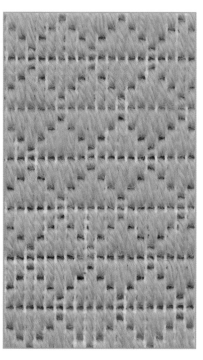

Long stitch (p177)

Stitch gallery

CROSSED STITCHES

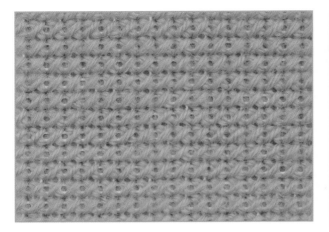

Cross stitch (p179)

Straight cross stitch (p179)

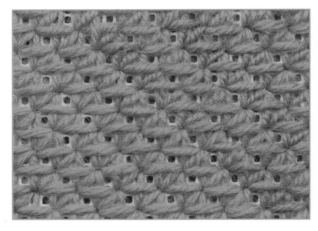

Diagonal cross stitch (p180)

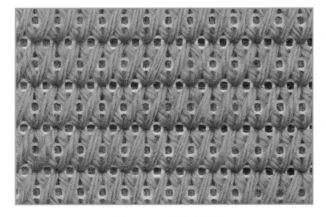

Oblong cross stitch (p180)

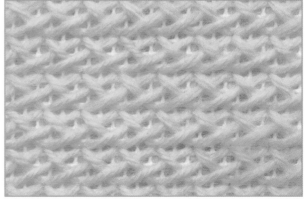

Long-armed cross stitch (p181)

Stitch gallery

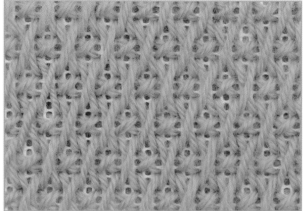

Alternating cross stitch (p182)

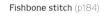

Fishbone stitch (p184)

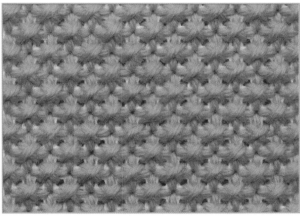

Double straight cross stitch (p182)

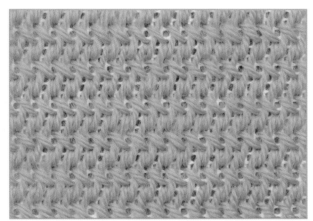

Knotted stitch (p185)

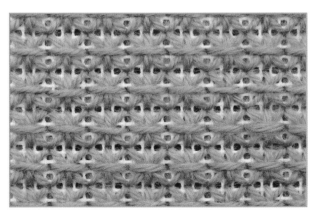

Smyrna stitch (p183)

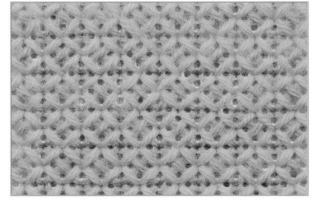

Rice stitch (p186)

LOOP STITCHES

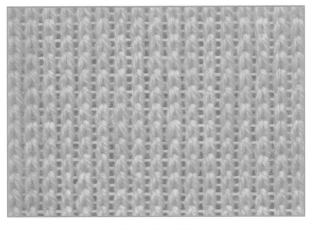

Chain stitch (p186)

Pile stitch (p187)

STAR STITCHES

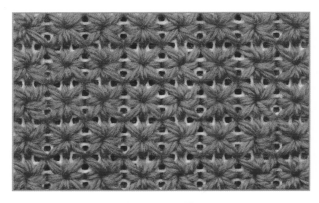

Star stitch (p188)

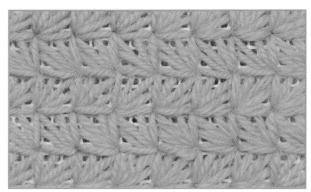

Fan stitch (p189)

Diamond eyelet stitch (p190)

Leaf stitch (p191)

Bargello or Florentine work

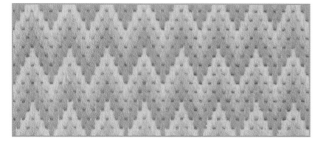

Basic bargello stitch (p202)

Hungarian point (p205)

Pomegranate (p210)

Undulating stripes (p211)

Flame stitch (p211)

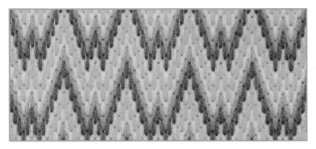

Ws (p211)

Lattice (p211)

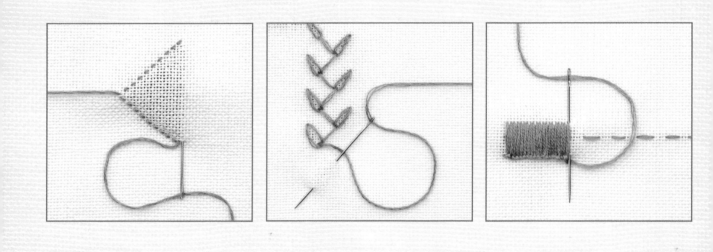

EMBROIDERY
BASICS

Embroidery basics

Embroidery stitches can be used to add decorative stitches or embellishments to items of clothing, accessories, or home furnishings. Before you start your embroidery you need to prepare your fabric, designs, and threads. Find a suitably sized hoop or frame and mount your fabric. Once you have chosen and transferred your design, you should organize your threads, preparing skeins, if required.

Using hoops and frames

Before using a hoop or frame you need to prepare and mount the fabric that you will embroider onto. The inner ring of a hoop should be bound with woven cotton tape, both to protect the fabric and to help keep it taut. Make sure the fabric is larger than the hoop and, if possible, that the hoop is larger than the area to be stitched. To mount on a frame, hem or bind the edges of the fabric and attach with herringbone stitch (see page 74).

BINDING A HOOP

Secure the end of a length of cotton tape inside the inner hoop and wrap it around the ring, overlapping as you work. Secure the ends with a few stitches.

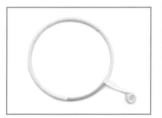

MOUNTING FABRIC IN A HOOP

1 Center the fabric over the bound inner ring and place the outer ring on it. Hemming or binding the edges of the fabric will help to prevent it from fraying as you work.

2 Press the outer ring around the inner one and tighten the tension screw slowly to hold the rings together and the fabric taut and even. Smooth any wrinkles before tightening.

Transferring embroidery designs and patterns

Designs and patterns for embroidery are everywhere—in nature, in geometry, in our imaginations—and transferring them to fabric is not difficult. Many items such as pillow covers and table linens are available with a design already marked. Magazines and books are good sources for patterns, or you can draw your own.

DIRECT TRACING

Good for thin, light-colored fabrics. Anchor the pattern on your work surface. Place the fabric on top, securing it with tape or thumbtacks. Draw over the lines with a sharp pencil or water-soluble marker.

USING A LIGHTBOX

Another good method for transferring motifs to light-colored solid weaves. Place the pattern on a lightbox, with the fabric on top, and draw over the lines with a sharp pencil or water-soluble marker.

DRESSMAKER'S CARBON PAPER

Use on fabrics that are too dark to see through. Place the fabric right-side up with the carbon paper on top. Place the design on top of the carbon paper. Draw over the lines with a sharp pencil.

IRON-ON TRANSFERS

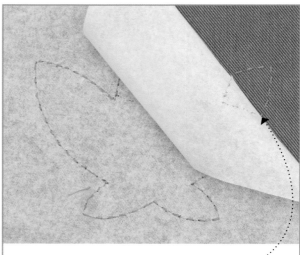

Follow the manufacturer's instructions to apply transfers.

BASTE-AND-TEAR METHOD

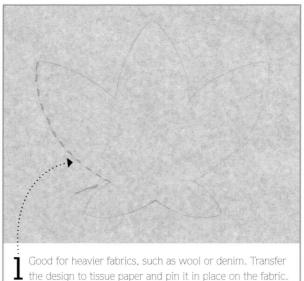

1 Good for heavier fabrics, such as wool or denim. Transfer the design to tissue paper and pin it in place on the fabric. With the knot on top, sew along the pattern lines with a small running stitch. Secure the end with a double backstitch.

2 Pull the paper away gently without disturbing the basting. If necessary, score the marked lines with a pinpoint to break the paper.

Embroidery basics

Preparing the thread

It is useful to know a few tricks of the trade before you start embroidering, from learning how to unwind a skein of thread to separating strands of embroidery floss. Most embroidery floss comes in specially wound hanks or skeins designed by the spinners to make them easier to work with, but they need special handling to keep them from becoming tangled.

LOOPED SKEINS

Do not remove looped skeins, such as stranded floss, from their paper bands. Inside one end of the skein is a loose end of thread. Hold the other end of the skein and gently pull out the loose thread.

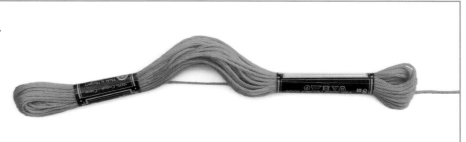

TWISTED SKEINS

Unwrap twisted skeins, such as pearl cotton. Free the hank and cut across the threads, to give cut threads the right length for working. Slip the paper band back on and tie the threads loosely.

SEPARATING STRANDS

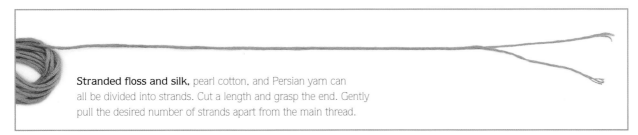

Stranded floss and silk, pearl cotton, and Persian yarn can all be divided into strands. Cut a length and grasp the end. Gently pull the desired number of strands apart from the main thread.

Threading a needle

Work with a length of thread of less than 18in (50cm), unless the technique calls for a longer one. Most embroidery threads are thicker than ordinary sewing thread and, although the eyes of crewel and tapestry needles are large, they can sometimes be difficult to thread. Finer threads can be inserted using a needle threader. Use the folding method shown here for thicker types.

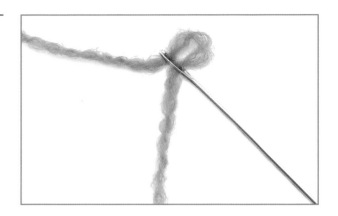

Fold the thread over the eye of the needle and hold the loop tight. Slide it off the end of the needle and into the eye.

Starting and finishing

On most embroideries, knots are undesirable, since they make a bump under the fabric and can sometimes show through. There are other ways to secure the beginning and end of your stitching. The method you choose will depend on the thread, fabric, and design as well as the stitches you use.

LEAVING A TAIL OF THREAD

Leave a tail of 2in (5cm) of thread on the back when you start, and weave it into the stitching upon completion (see Finishing off, opposite).

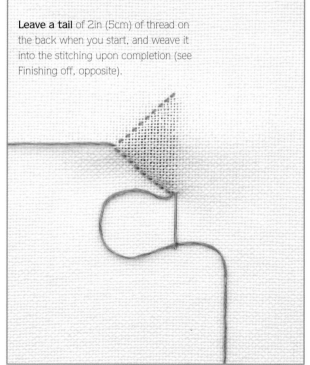

LOST KNOT METHOD

1 Knot the thread and insert the needle from front to back, at least 1in (2.5cm) from where you want to start, leaving the knot on the front. Run the thread along the back, to where you want to start.

2 Work the first few stitches toward the knot, covering the thread on the back to hold it in place. When the stitching is complete, cut the knot and any tail of thread.

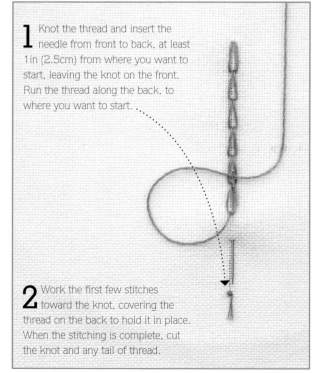

BACKSTITCH METHOD

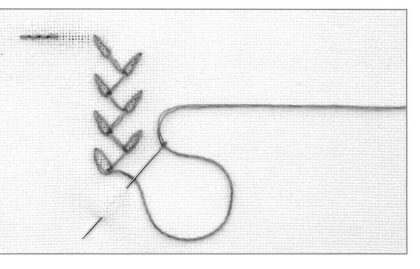

About 1in (2.5cm) from where you want to begin, take the needle from front to back, leaving a 2in (5cm) tail. Work 2 or 3 backstitches to the start. Complete the embroidery, take out the backstitches, and run in the tail on the wrong side, under the first stitches.

RUNNING-STITCH METHOD

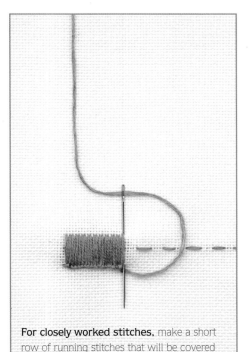

For closely worked stitches, make a short row of running stitches that will be covered by the embroidery. Leave a loose tail of thread on the back and weave on the reverse side when completed.

FINISHING OFF

Finish a thread by weaving it under a group of stitches for at least 2–3in (5–7cm) on the back and cutting the thread. Fasten off before the thread is too short to slide under.

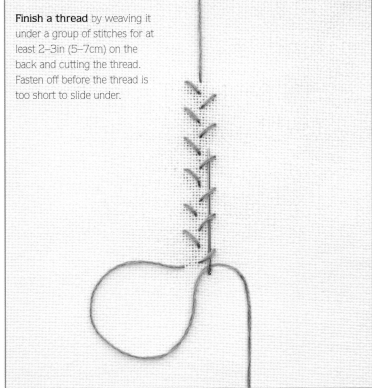

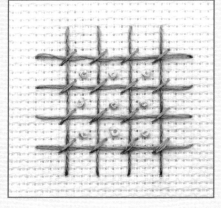

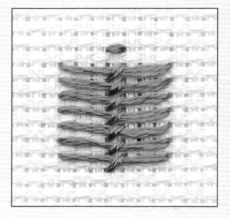

SURFACE
EMBROIDERY

Surface embroidery

Decorating fabrics with embroidery is a satisfying way to make something unique, be it an article of clothing or an item for the home. Stitching the surface of cloth, whether the work is simple or complex, adds texture and interest, and can be done on virtually any fabric. Plain-weave, or common-weave, fabrics are most often used for surface embellishment, but many household textiles or accessories can be made from even-weave cloth and embroidered.

Cross stitch

These stitches can stand alone or be worked in rows. To work rows of stitches, complete the row of diagonal stitches from right to left, then reverse the direction to complete the cross stitches.

INDIVIDUAL CROSS STITCH

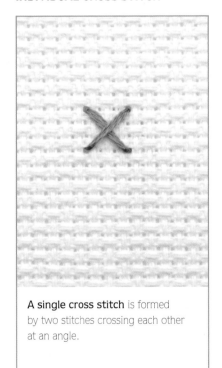

A single cross stitch is formed by two stitches crossing each other at an angle.

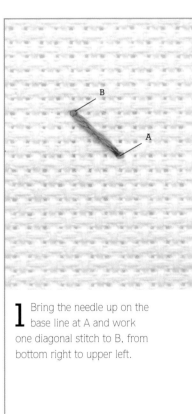

1 Bring the needle up on the base line at A and work one diagonal stitch to B, from bottom right to upper left.

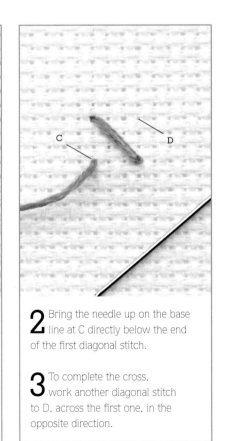

2 Bring the needle up on the base line at C directly below the end of the first diagonal stitch.

3 To complete the cross, work another diagonal stitch to D, across the first one, in the opposite direction.

SERIAL CROSS STITCH

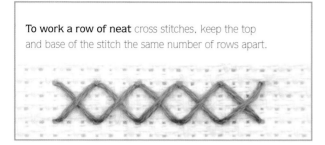

To work a row of neat cross stitches, keep the top and base of the stitch the same number of rows apart.

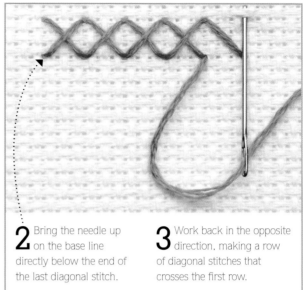

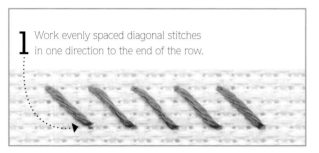

1 Work evenly spaced diagonal stitches in one direction to the end of the row.

2 Bring the needle up on the base line directly below the end of the last diagonal stitch.

3 Work back in the opposite direction, making a row of diagonal stitches that crosses the first row.

DOUBLE-SIDED STITCH

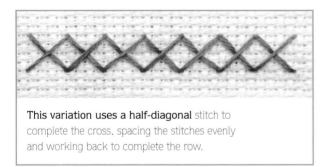

This variation uses a half-diagonal stitch to complete the cross, spacing the stitches evenly and working back to complete the row.

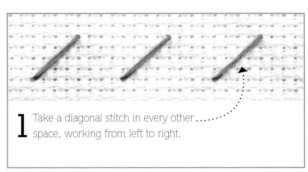

1 Take a diagonal stitch in every other space, working from left to right.

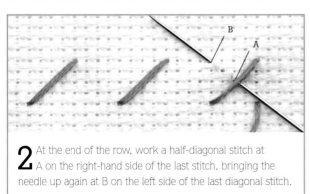

2 At the end of the row, work a half-diagonal stitch at A on the right-hand side of the last stitch, bringing the needle up again at B on the left side of the last diagonal stitch.

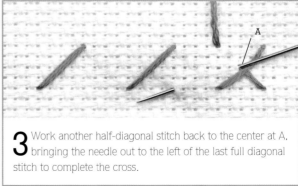

3 Work another half-diagonal stitch back to the center at A, bringing the needle out to the left of the last full diagonal stitch to complete the cross.

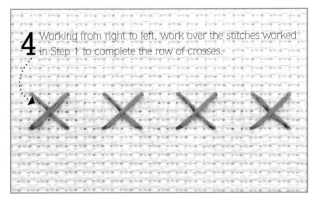

4 Working from right to left, work over the stitches worked in Step 1 to complete the row of crosses.

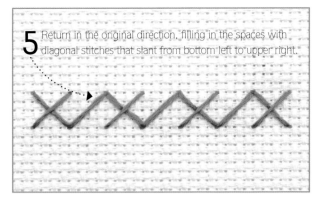

5 Return in the original direction, filling in the spaces with diagonal stitches that slant from bottom left to upper right.

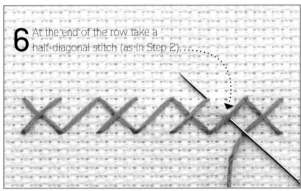

6 At the end of the row take a half-diagonal stitch (as in Step 2).

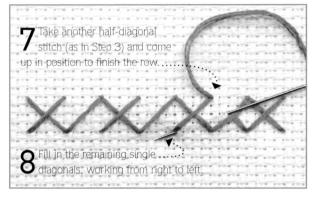

7 Take another half-diagonal stitch (as in Step 3) and come up in position to finish the row.

8 Fill in the remaining single diagonals, working from right to left.

LONG-ARMED CROSS STITCH

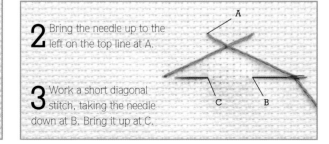

This stitch is useful for borders. Keep the proportion of twice as many vertical threads as horizontal ones as you work.

1 Work a long diagonal stitch from left to right over an even number of vertical threads and half as many horizontal ones.

2 Bring the needle up to the left on the top line at A.

3 Work a short diagonal stitch, taking the needle down at B. Bring it up at C.

Surface embroidery

ST. GEORGE CROSS STITCH

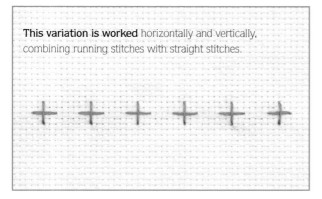

This variation is worked horizontally and vertically, combining running stitches with straight stitches.

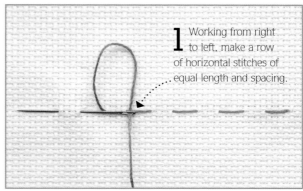

1 Working from right to left, make a row of horizontal stitches of equal length and spacing.

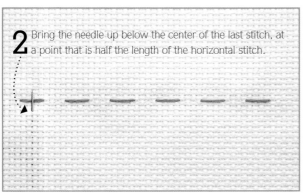

2 Bring the needle up below the center of the last stitch, at a point that is half the length of the horizontal stitch.

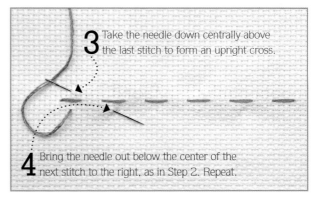

3 Take the needle down centrally above the last stitch to form an upright cross.

4 Bring the needle out below the center of the next stitch to the right, as in Step 2. Repeat.

Flat stitches

Flat stitches have an almost flat texture. There are a number of filling stitches (see pages 76–80) that are similar to the flat-stitch family but are more three-dimensional. The stitches shown here are all based on straight stitch.

STRAIGHT STITCH

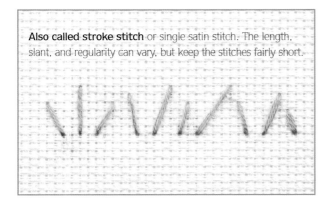

Also called stroke stitch or single satin stitch. The length, slant, and regularity can vary, but keep the stitches fairly short.

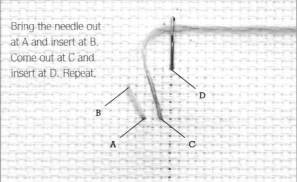

Bring the needle out at A and insert at B. Come out at C and insert at D. Repeat.

LONG AND SHORT STITCH

Also called shading stitch. The first row consists of alternate short and long stitches, but subsequent rows are filled with stitches of the same length.

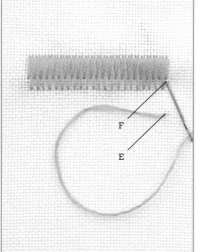

1 Bring the needle out at A and insert at B.

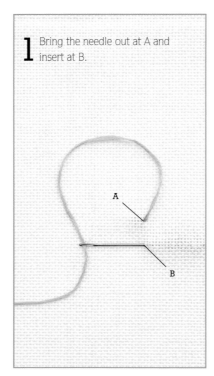

2 Make the next stitch longer. Bring the needle out at C and insert it next to B, at D. Repeat the short-and-long sequence along the foundation row, placing stitches as close together as possible.

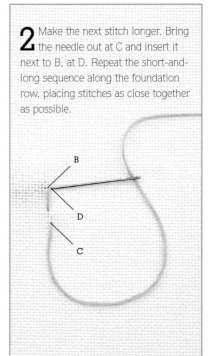

3 To work the next row, bring the needle out at E, below a short stitch, and insert it at F, almost touching the thread above.

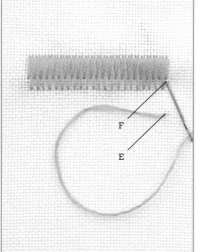

4 Repeat, coming out at G and down at H, making the stitch the same length as in Step 3. Repeat to fill the design.

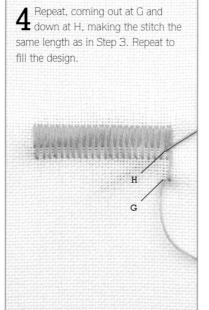

BLENDING COLORS

Changing the thread to different tones of the same color will give blended effects.

Surface embroidery

LEAF STITCH

Leaf stitch is often used to create leaf shapes with a central spine and pretty veins, but it can also work well as a border stitch.

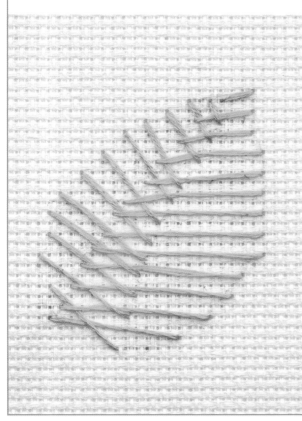

1 Draw 2 guidelines through the center of the motif that meet at the top and gradually diverge. Bring the needle out at A, at the bottom of the left-hand inner line, and insert it at B, on the right-hand edge.

2 Come out at C, on the right-hand inner line, and insert at D, on the left-hand edge.

3 Come out at E, on the left-hand inner line, below the previous stitch D. Insert at F, leaving a space above the first stitch.

4 Continue, spacing evenly, until the shape is filled.

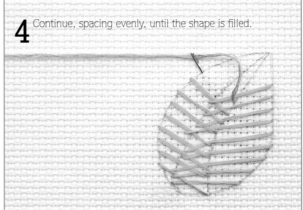

FERN STITCH

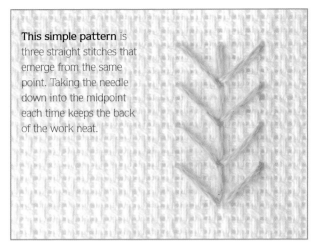

This simple pattern is three straight stitches that emerge from the same point. Taking the needle down into the midpoint each time keeps the back of the work neat.

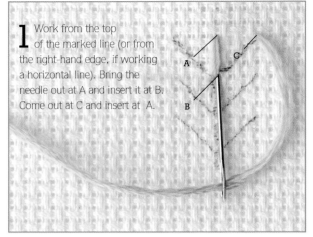

1 Work from the top of the marked line (or from the right-hand edge, if working a horizontal line). Bring the needle out at A and insert it at B. Come out at C and insert at A.

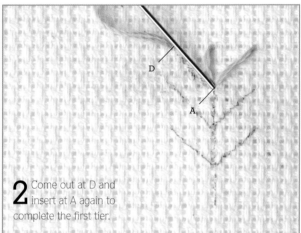

2 Come out at D and insert at A again to complete the first tier.

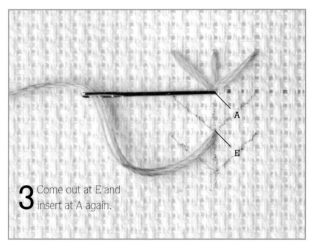

3 Come out at E and insert at A again.

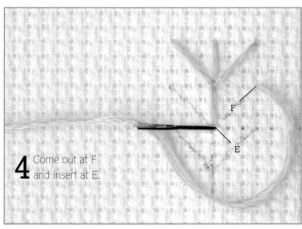

4 Come out at F and insert at E.

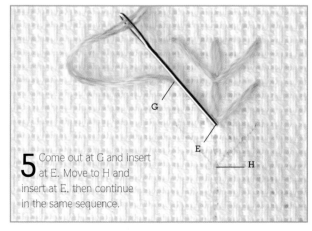

5 Come out at G and insert at E. Move to H and insert at E, then continue in the same sequence.

Outline stitches

As the name implies, outline stitches are used to delineate the edge of a motif. They can look simple or complex, but all are straightforward to work.

RUNNING STITCH

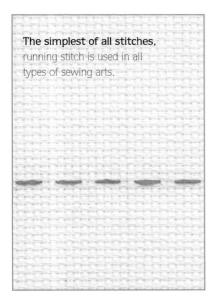

The simplest of all stitches, running stitch is used in all types of sewing arts.

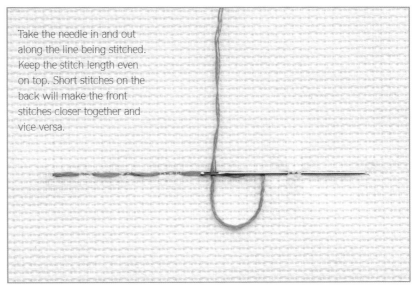

Take the needle in and out along the line being stitched. Keep the stitch length even on top. Short stitches on the back will make the front stitches closer together and vice versa.

LACED RUNNING STITCH

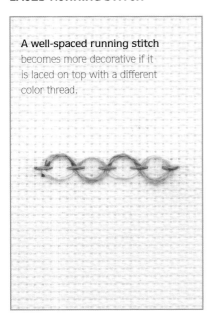

A well-spaced running stitch becomes more decorative if it is laced on top with a different color thread.

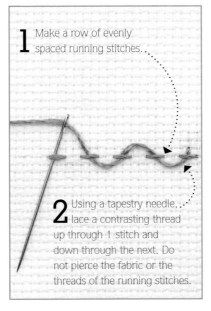

1 Make a row of evenly spaced running stitches.

2 Using a tapestry needle, lace a contrasting thread up through 1 stitch and down through the next. Do not pierce the fabric or the threads of the running stitches.

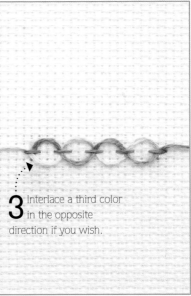

3 Interlace a third color in the opposite direction if you wish.

STEM STITCH

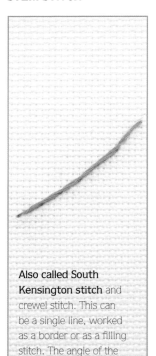

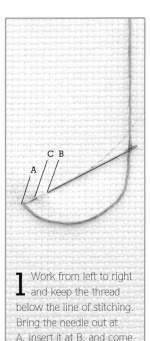

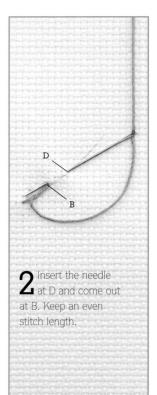

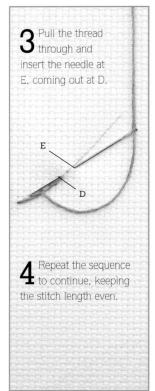

3 Pull the thread through and insert the needle at E, coming out at D.

Also called South Kensington stitch and crewel stitch. This can be a single line, worked as a border or as a filling stitch. The angle of the needle determines the width of the outline.

1 Work from left to right and keep the thread below the line of stitching. Bring the needle out at A, insert it at B, and come out again at C, about halfway back toward A.

2 Insert the needle at D and come out at B. Keep an even stitch length.

4 Repeat the sequence to continue, keeping the stitch length even.

BACKSTITCH

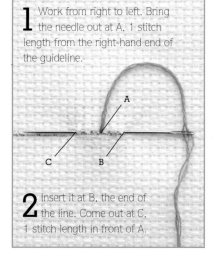

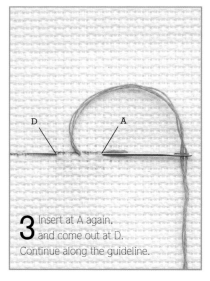

Backstitch creates a straight line without the spacing of running stitch.

1 Work from right to left. Bring the needle out at A, 1 stitch length from the right-hand end of the guideline.

2 Insert it at B, the end of the line. Come out at C, 1 stitch length in front of A.

3 Insert at A again, and come out at D. Continue along the guideline.

WHIPPED BACKSTITCH

Whipping an outline stitch with a matching or contrasting thread gives it extra texture.

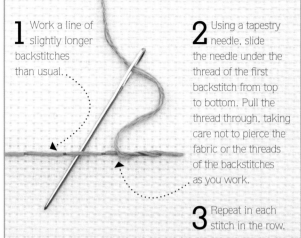

1 Work a line of slightly longer backstitches than usual.

2 Using a tapestry needle, slide the needle under the thread of the first backstitch from top to bottom. Pull the thread through, taking care not to pierce the fabric or the threads of the backstitches as you work.

3 Repeat in each stitch in the row.

PEKINESE STITCH

Also known as forbidden stitch, Pekinese stitch is found on ancient Chinese embroideries. It is particularly effective worked with silk or metallic threads as a border.

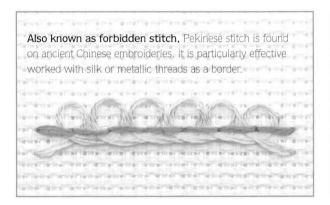

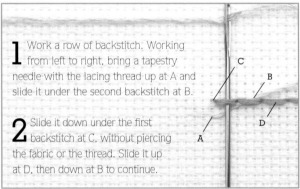

1 Work a row of backstitch. Working from left to right, bring a tapestry needle with the lacing thread up at A and slide it under the second backstitch at B.

2 Slide it down under the first backstitch at C, without piercing the fabric or the thread. Slide it up at D, then down at B to continue.

HOLBEIN STITCH

Also known as double running stitch, Holbein stitch is neater when worked on even-weave fabric. It is normally worked with 1 thread; here, for clarity, a contrasting color has been used for the return stitches.

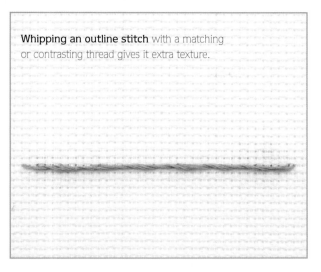

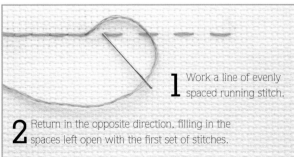

1 Work a line of evenly spaced running stitch.

2 Return in the opposite direction, filling in the spaces left open with the first set of stitches.

SPLIT STITCH

Work split stitch with a fine needle and stranded floss or soft crewel yarn for the best results.

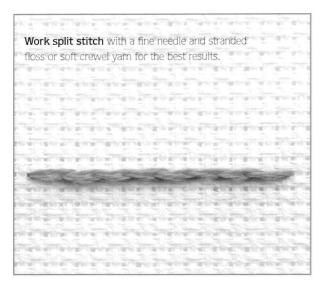

1 Working from left to right, bring the needle up at A and down at B. Bring the needle out at C, splitting the first stitch in the middle.

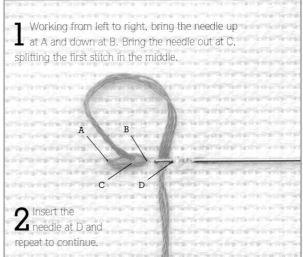

2 Insert the needle at D and repeat to continue.

HERRINGBONE STITCH

Herringbone stitch is a basic outline stitch that also works well as a border. If you are working on plain-weave fabric, mark 2 parallel guidelines.

1 Bring the needle out at A, on the bottom guideline.

2 Take a diagonal stitch to the top guideline. Insert the needle at B and bring it out a short stitch back at C.

3 Take a diagonal stitch in the opposite direction along the bottom guideline, inserting the needle at D and coming out at E.

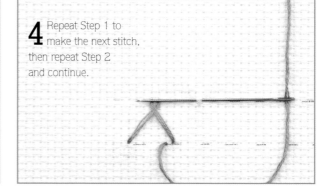

4 Repeat Step 1 to make the next stitch, then repeat Step 2 and continue.

CLOSED HERRINGBONE STITCH

Also known as double backstitch when worked on the front. This is a heavily textured stitch that can also be used as a border.

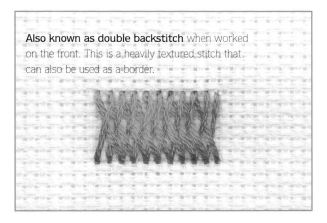

Work as for herringbone stitch, opposite, but place the stitches next to each other. The tops and bottoms of the diagonal stitches should touch each other.

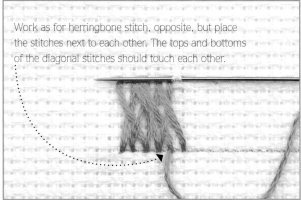

CHEVRON STITCH

Chevron stitch is another outline stitch that also works well as a border. If you work on plain-weave fabric, mark 2 parallel guidelines.

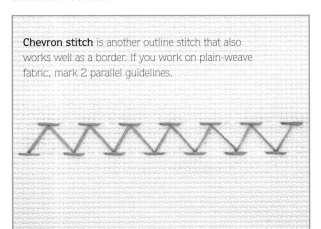

1 Bring the needle up at A on the bottom guideline and insert it at B. Come out at C.

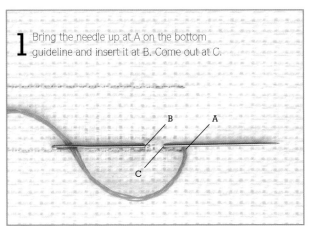

2 Insert the needle at D on the top guideline and come out a little to the left, at E. Bring the thread through to make a horizontal stitch along the top.

3 Insert the needle at F and bring it out again at D.

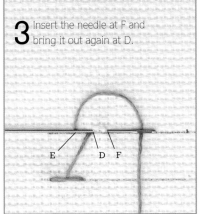

4 Insert the needle at G on the bottom guideline, and bring it out at H.

5 Insert it a little to the right, at J, and bring it out again at G.

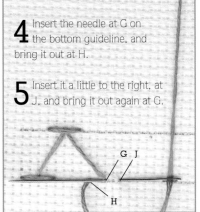

Filling stitches

Almost any stitch can be used to fill an area of background, but some are more effective and useful than others. Filling can be worked solidly, like satin stitch, or lightly, like dot stitch, depending on the effect you want to create.

DOT STITCH

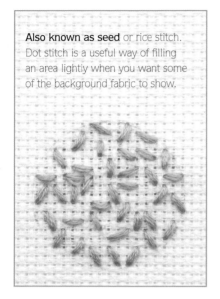

Also known as seed or rice stitch. Dot stitch is a useful way of filling an area lightly when you want some of the background fabric to show.

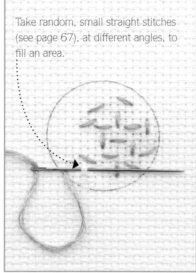

Take random, small straight stitches (see page 67), at different angles, to fill an area.

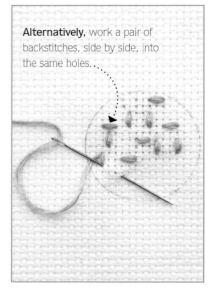

Alternatively, work a pair of backstitches, side by side, into the same holes.

SHEAF STITCH

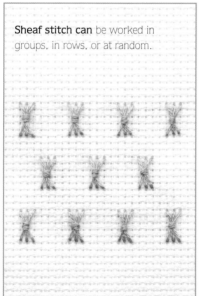

Sheaf stitch can be worked in groups, in rows, or at random.

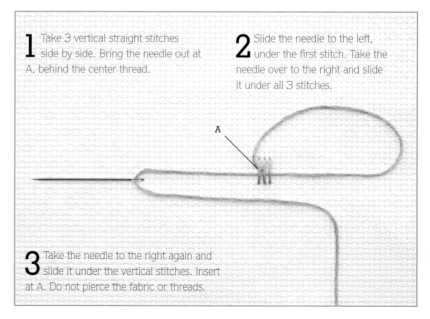

1 Take 3 vertical straight stitches side by side. Bring the needle out at A, behind the center thread.

2 Slide the needle to the left, under the first stitch. Take the needle over to the right and slide it under all 3 stitches.

3 Take the needle to the right again and slide it under the vertical stitches. Insert at A. Do not pierce the fabric or threads.

SPIDER'S WEB

Threads woven in and out of an odd-numbered foundation of evenly spaced spokes makes a webbed wheel.

1 Mark a circular outline if using plain-weave fabric. Bring the needle out at A and insert it at B. Come out in the center, at C.

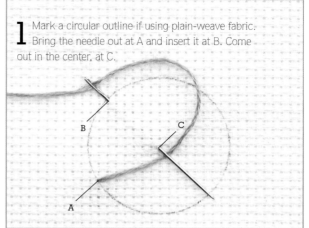

2 Catching the thread under in the center, insert the needle at D on the other side. Come up at E, halfway between D and A.

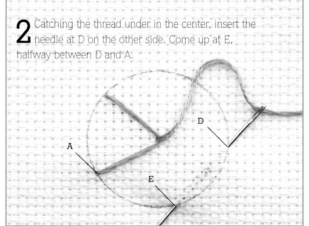

3 Take the needle back to C and insert in the center, coming up at F, halfway between B and D. Take it back and insert at C.

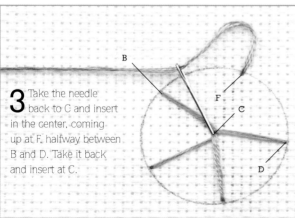

4 Bring a thread to the front and use a tapestry needle to weave under and over through the spokes to fill the circle. Do not pierce the fabric or split the spoke threads.

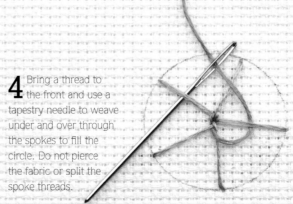

SATIN STITCH

Satin stitch is a popular basic filling stitch. Use a hoop to keep your stitching smooth and even.

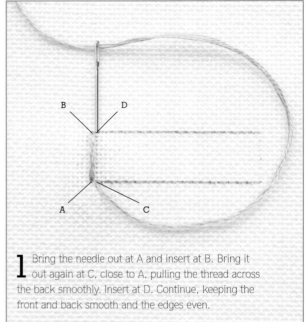

1 Bring the needle out at A and insert at B. Bring it out again at C, close to A, pulling the thread across the back smoothly. Insert at D. Continue, keeping the front and back smooth and the edges even.

PADDED SATIN STITCH

To give satin stitch a raised profile it can be padded with a foundation of running stitch. It is useful for creating elegant monograms.

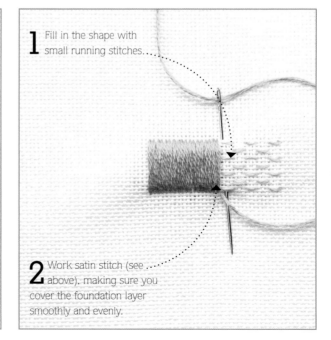

1 Fill in the shape with small running stitches.

2 Work satin stitch (see above), making sure you cover the foundation layer smoothly and evenly.

Surface embroidery

WHIPPED SATIN STITCH

Whipped satin stitch adds texture that contrasts with plain satin stitch.

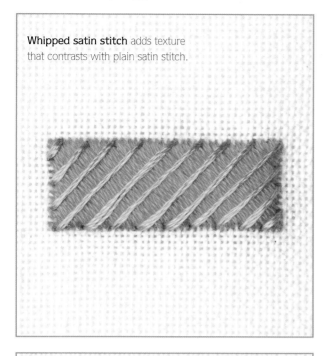

Cover the shape with satin stitch worked on a diagonal. Come out at A, slightly below the beginning of the shape. Insert the needle at B, slanting the stitch on the opposite diagonal. Continue, spacing the stitches across the shape.

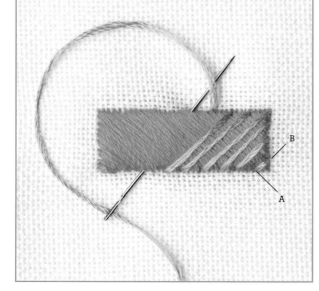

FLAT STITCH

Flat stitch is closely worked and should be worked in a hoop or frame. It is ideal for making leaves and flowers.

1 Mark the center of the shape with 2 internal guidelines, as shown.

2 Bring the needle out at A, on the outside edge, and insert at B, near the top of the left-hand center guideline. Come out at C, on the left-hand outside edge, and insert at D, on the right-hand center guideline.

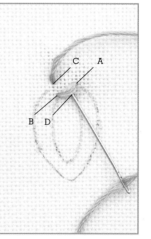

3 Come out at E, next to A, and cross to F, on the left-hand center guideline next to the stitch.

4 Repeat Steps 2–3 to continue.

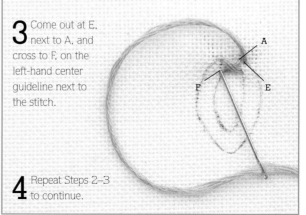

Surface embroidery

FISHBONE STITCH

This variation on flat stitch overlaps along a single center guideline, resulting in a more acute angle.

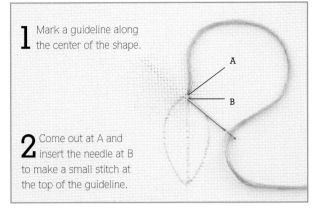

1 Mark a guideline along the center of the shape.

2 Come out at A and insert the needle at B to make a small stitch at the top of the guideline.

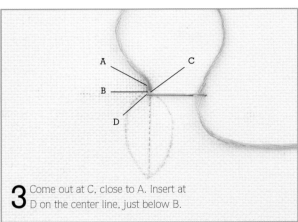

3 Come out at C, close to A. Insert at D on the center line, just below B.

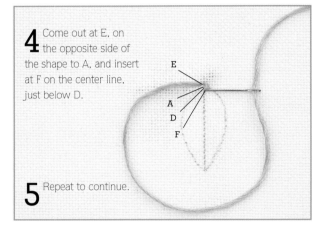

4 Come out at E, on the opposite side of the shape to A, and insert at F on the center line, just below D.

5 Repeat to continue.

DARNING STITCH

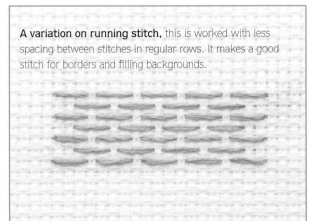

A variation on running stitch, this is worked with less spacing between stitches in regular rows. It makes a good stitch for borders and filling backgrounds.

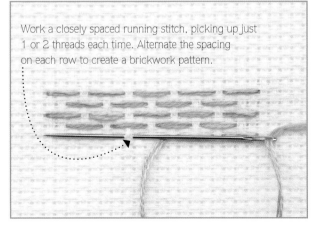

Work a closely spaced running stitch, picking up just 1 or 2 threads each time. Alternate the spacing on each row to create a brickwork pattern.

Looped stitches

Looped stitches are all based on looping a thread around the needle before securing it. Many of them can be used as outline or border stitches, while others can fill in shapes or occur in isolation.

BUTTONHOLE STITCH AND BLANKET STITCH

Both of these stitches are worked the same way, from left to right. They differ only in the spacing between each vertical stitch.

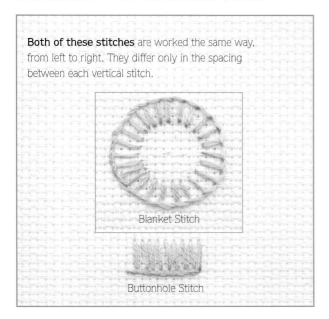

Blanket Stitch

Buttonhole Stitch

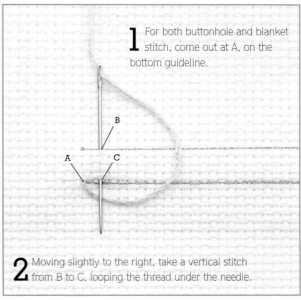

1 For both buttonhole and blanket stitch, come out at A, on the bottom guideline.

2 Moving slightly to the right, take a vertical stitch from B to C, looping the thread under the needle.

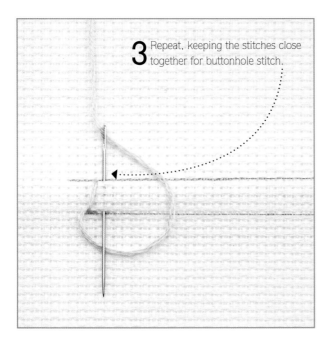

3 Repeat, keeping the stitches close together for buttonhole stitch.

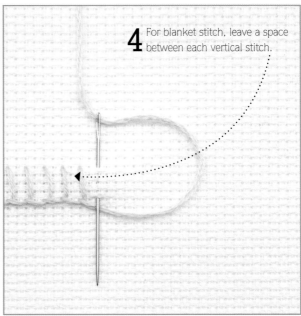

4 For blanket stitch, leave a space between each vertical stitch.

CLOSED BUTTONHOLE STITCH

In this variation on blanket stitch, the vertical stitches are worked in pairs and slanted to form inverted V-shapes.

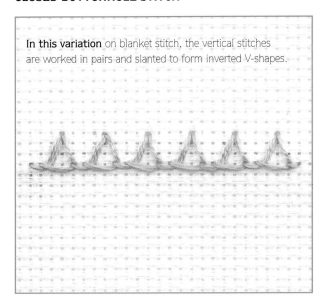

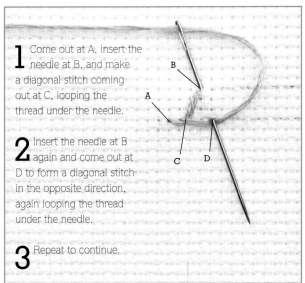

1 Come out at A, insert the needle at B, and make a diagonal stitch coming out at C, looping the thread under the needle.

2 Insert the needle at B again and come out at D to form a diagonal stitch in the opposite direction, again looping the thread under the needle.

3 Repeat to continue.

KNOTTED BUTTONHOLE STITCH

A decorative knot is formed at the top of each vertical stitch in this variation.

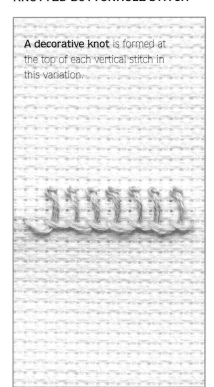

1 Come up at A, loop the thread counterclockwise (from right to left) over your working thumb, and insert the needle into the loop from below.

2 Insert the needle at B and come out at C, with the thread under the point of the needle.

3 Pull the thread taut to create a knot and loop the thread around your thumb, as in Step 1.

4 Repeat the stitch, then repeat Steps 1–3 to continue.

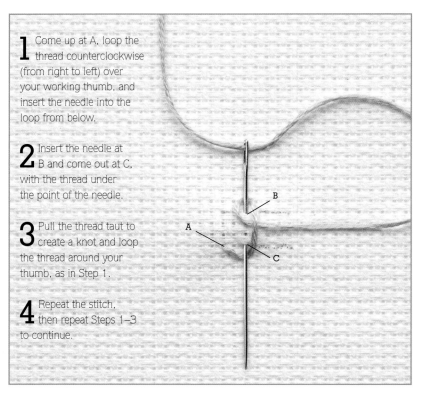

Surface embroidery

DOUBLE BUTTONHOLE STITCH

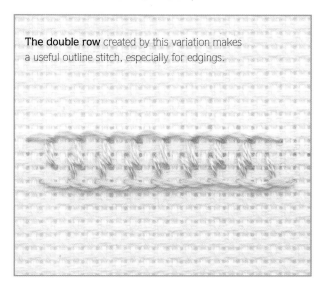

The double row created by this variation makes a useful outline stitch, especially for edgings.

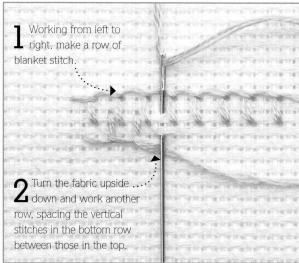

1 Working from left to right, make a row of blanket stitch.

2 Turn the fabric upside down and work another row, spacing the vertical stitches in the bottom row between those in the top.

FEATHER STITCH

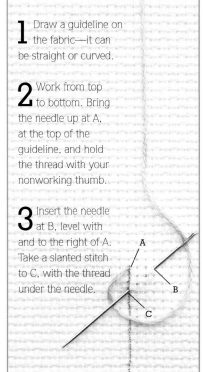

Also called briar stitch and coral stitch. Feather stitch is often used to decorate the seams on crazy quilts and to outline appliqué motifs, as well as making feathery patterns for embroidery.

1 Draw a guideline on the fabric—it can be straight or curved.

2 Work from top to bottom. Bring the needle up at A, at the top of the guideline, and hold the thread with your nonworking thumb.

3 Insert the needle at B, level with and to the right of A. Take a slanted stitch to C, with the thread under the needle.

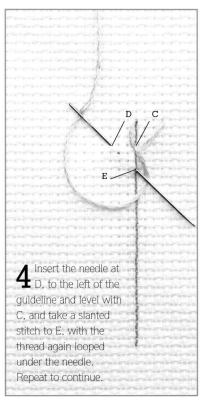

4 Insert the needle at D, to the left of the guideline and level with C, and take a slanted stitch to E, with the thread again looped under the needle. Repeat to continue.

SINGLE FEATHER STITCH

Single feather stitch
is worked like feather
stitch, but the loops are
positioned on only one
side of the guideline.

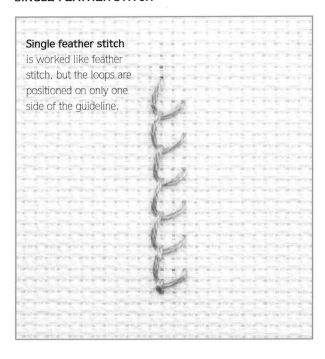

1 Work from top to bottom. Bring the
needle out at A at the top of the guideline
and insert it at B, below A and to the right of
the guideline.

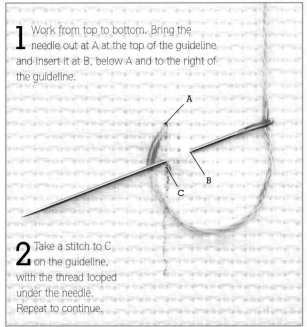

2 Take a stitch to C
on the guideline,
with the thread looped
under the needle.
Repeat to continue.

DOUBLE FEATHER STITCH

In this variation
on feather stitch, extra
stitches are made on
each side of the line to
fill a broader area. Use
a hoop to stretch the
fabric taut.

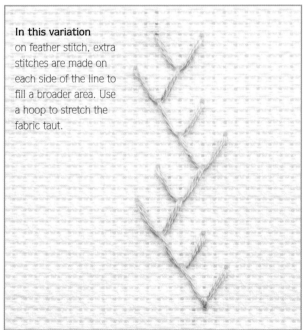

Work as for feather stitch (see
page 83), working from top to
bottom and alternating from left to
right—but on each side of the first
stitch make 2 or more stitches.

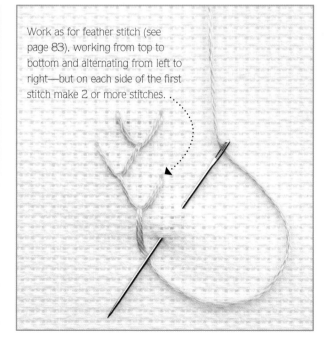

Surface embroidery

CLOSED FEATHER STITCH

This variation on feather stitch is a useful border or outline stitch that can also be used for couching (see page 97). As with feather stitch, work from top to bottom.

1 Mark 2 parallel guidelines and bring the needle up at A, at the top of one line. Insert the needle at B and bring it up at C on the opposite guideline, looping the thread under the needle.

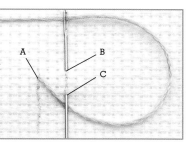

2 Insert the needle at D, below A on the first guideline, and come out at E, again looping the thread under the needle and parallel to the previous stitch. Repeat to continue.

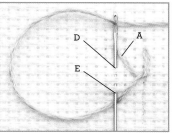

LOOP STITCH

Like many looped stitches, loop stitch is usually worked in straight lines. The looping creates a raised knot in the center of each stitch with two "legs," which give the stitch its other name of centipede stitch.

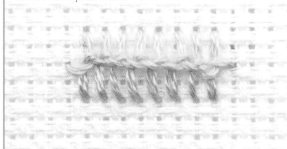

1 Mark 2 parallel guidelines on the fabric and work from right to left. Bring the needle out in the center at A, in between the marked lines. Insert it diagonally at B on the top line and come out at C, directly below B between the guidelines. Take the needle under the stitch (A–B) and over the working thread.

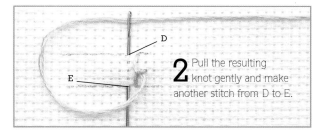

2 Pull the resulting knot gently and make another stitch from D to E.

3 Again, take the needle under the stitch and over the working thread. Repeat to continue.

VANDYKE STITCH

Vandyke stitch, with its braided look, can be used as a border or as a filling stitch.

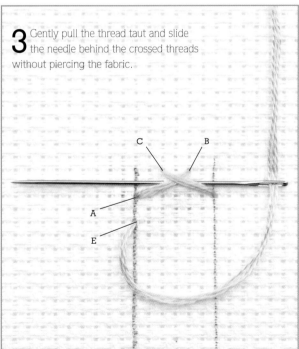

1 Work from top to bottom along parallel guidelines. Bring the needle out at A, on the left-hand guideline. Insert it at B, slightly above A and midway between the guidelines, and bring it out at C, slightly to the left of B.

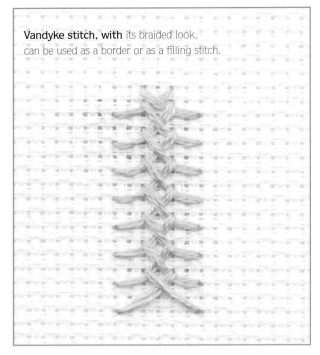

2 Take a stitch across A–B, inserting the needle level with A at D on the right-hand guideline and coming out at E, below A on the left-hand guideline.

3 Gently pull the thread taut and slide the needle behind the crossed threads without piercing the fabric.

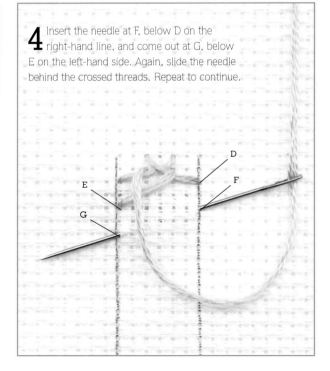

4 Insert the needle at F, below D on the right-hand line, and come out at G, below E on the left-hand side. Again, slide the needle behind the crossed threads. Repeat to continue.

CRETAN STITCH

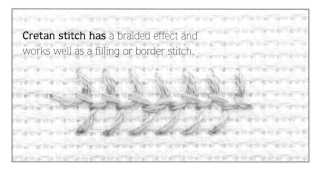

Cretan stitch has a braided effect and works well as a filling or border stitch.

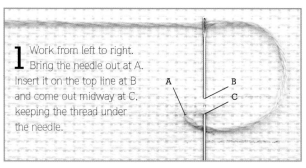

1 Work from left to right. Bring the needle out at A. Insert it on the top line at B and come out midway at C, keeping the thread under the needle.

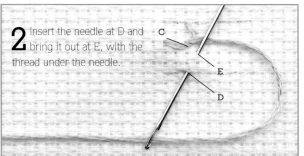

2 Insert the needle at D and bring it out at E, with the thread under the needle.

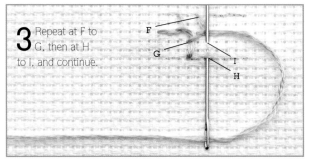

3 Repeat at F to G, then at H to I, and continue.

OPEN CRETAN STITCH

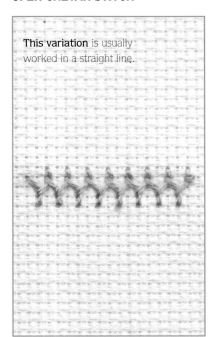

This variation is usually worked in a straight line.

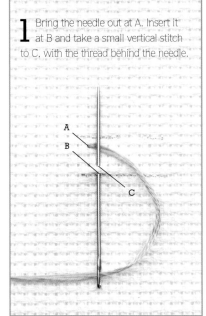

1 Bring the needle out at A. Insert it at B and take a small vertical stitch to C, with the thread behind the needle.

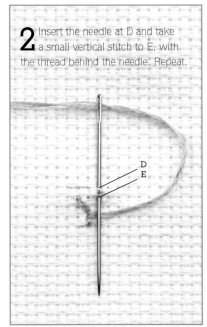

2 Insert the needle at D and take a small vertical stitch to E, with the thread behind the needle. Repeat.

FLY STITCH

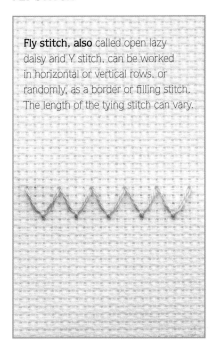

Fly stitch, also called open lazy daisy and Y stitch, can be worked in horizontal or vertical rows, or randomly, as a border or filling stitch. The length of the tying stitch can vary.

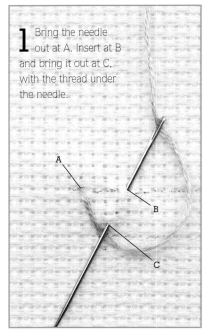

1 Bring the needle out at A. Insert at B and bring it out at C, with the thread under the needle.

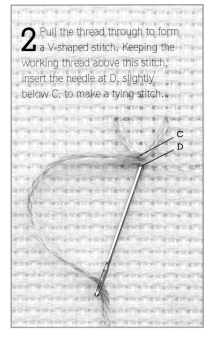

2 Pull the thread through to form a V-shaped stitch. Keeping the working thread above this stitch, insert the needle at D, slightly below C, to make a tying stitch.

BRAIDED FLY STITCH

In this variation the tails are longer and the arms overlap the next stitch. It can be worked in rows or randomly.

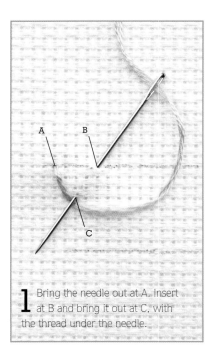

1 Bring the needle out at A. Insert at B and bring it out at C, with the thread under the needle.

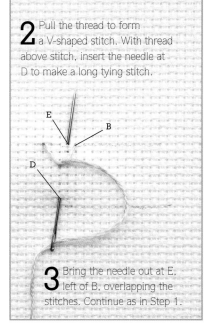

2 Pull the thread to form a V-shaped stitch. With thread above stitch, insert the needle at D to make a long tying stitch.

3 Bring the needle out at E, left of B, overlapping the stitches. Continue as in Step 1.

LADDER STITCH

Also known as step stitch. The loops at the side of the horizontal stitches give it the look of braid.

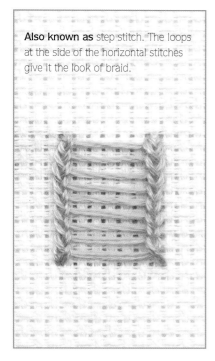

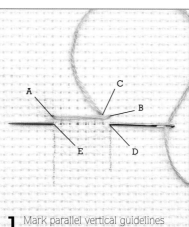

1 Mark parallel vertical guidelines on the fabric. Work from top to bottom. Bring the needle out at A. Insert it at B and bring it out at C, keeping the thread on top of the horizontal stitch. Insert the needle at D to form a short crossed stitch (C–D). Come out at E.

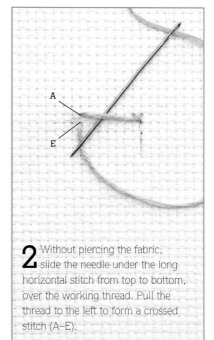

2 Without piercing the fabric, slide the needle under the long horizontal stitch from top to bottom, over the working thread. Pull the thread to the left to form a crossed stitch (A–E).

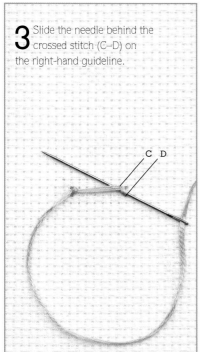

3 Slide the needle behind the crossed stitch (C–D) on the right-hand guideline.

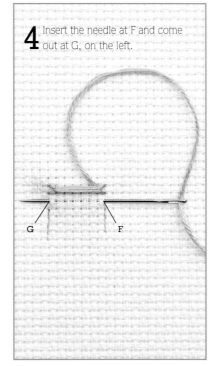

4 Insert the needle at F and come out at G, on the left.

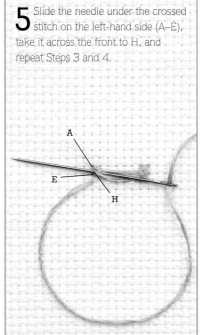

5 Slide the needle under the crossed stitch on the left-hand side (A–E), take it across the front to H, and repeat Steps 3 and 4.

Chained stitches

The stitches in this group are useful for borders, outlining, and filling. All except daisy stitch are worked as a continuous chain.

DAISY STITCH

Also known as lazy daisy or detached chain stitch, daisy stitch is simply a single chain stitch. It is often used to make flower petals.

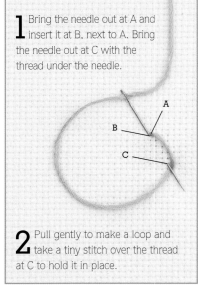

1 Bring the needle out at A and insert it at B, next to A. Bring the needle out at C with the thread under the needle.

2 Pull gently to make a loop and take a tiny stitch over the thread at C to hold it in place.

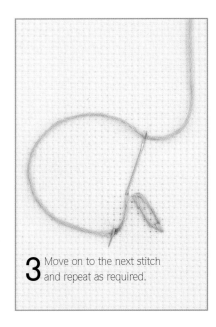

3 Move on to the next stitch and repeat as required.

CHAIN STITCH

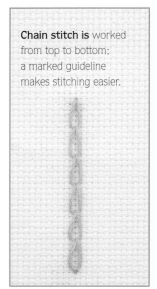

Chain stitch is worked from top to bottom; a marked guideline makes stitching easier.

1 Bring the needle up at A at the top of the line and insert it in the same hole. Hold the thread under the needle and come out below at B. Pull gently.

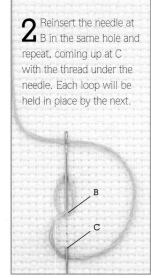

2 Reinsert the needle at B in the same hole and repeat, coming up at C with the thread under the needle. Each loop will be held in place by the next.

3 Tie the last loop in place by working a tiny stitch over the bottom of the loop.

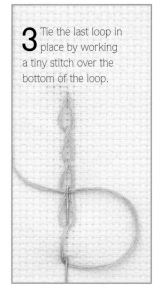

OPEN CHAIN STITCH

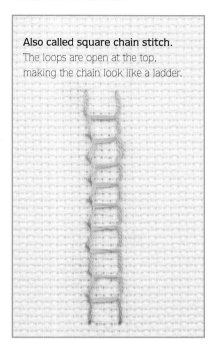

Also called square chain stitch. The loops are open at the top, making the chain look like a ladder.

1 Mark parallel guidelines. Bring the needle out at A, on the left. Insert the needle at B, on the right, and bring it out at C, below A. Keep the thread under the needle as you pull the stitch taut.

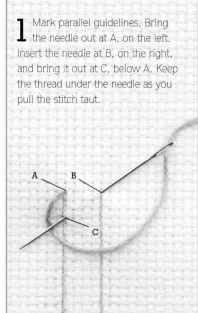

2 Insert the needle at D, inside the loop below B, and come out at E, below C—again with the thread under the needle. Repeat to continue.

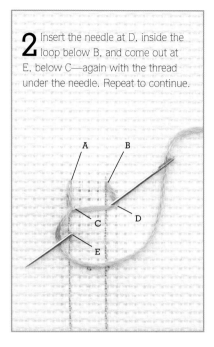

TWISTED CHAIN STITCH

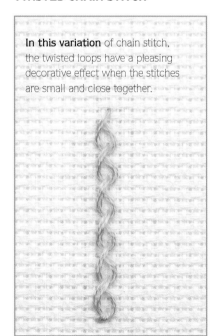

In this variation of chain stitch, the twisted loops have a pleasing decorative effect when the stitches are small and close together.

1 Come out at A, holding the thread below. Insert the needle at B, slightly to the left, come out at C, below A, with the thread under the needle.

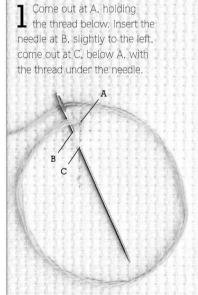

2 Again holding the thread, insert the needle at D, to the left of the line, and come out at E, with the thread under the needle. Make another twisted loop and continue.

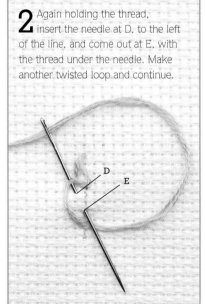

FEATHERED CHAIN STITCH

This chain stitch variation creates a zigzag line made of diagonal stitches with a chain loop at the top.

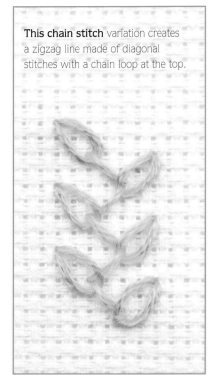

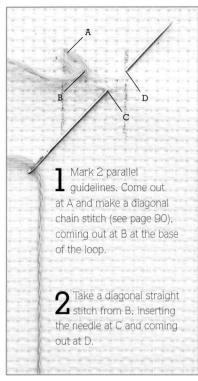

1 Mark 2 parallel guidelines. Come out at A and make a diagonal chain stitch (see page 90), coming out at B at the base of the loop.

2 Take a diagonal straight stitch from B, inserting the needle at C and coming out at D.

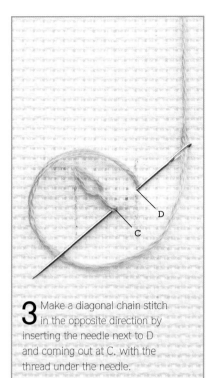

3 Make a diagonal chain stitch in the opposite direction by inserting the needle next to D and coming out at C, with the thread under the needle.

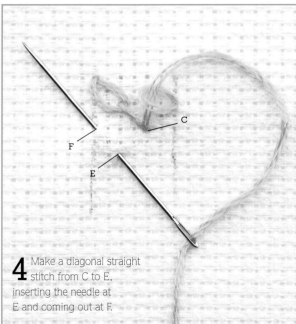

4 Make a diagonal straight stitch from C to E, inserting the needle at E and coming out at F.

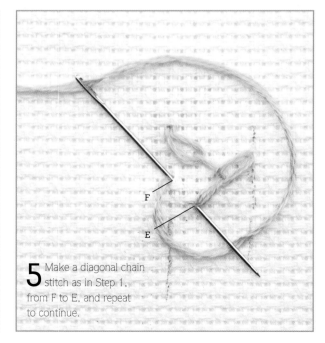

5 Make a diagonal chain stitch as in Step 1, from F to E, and repeat to continue.

WHEATEAR STITCH

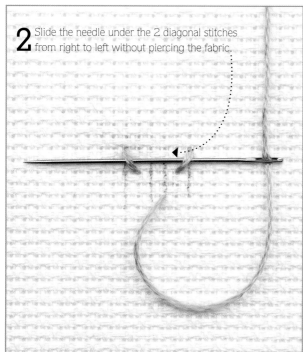

Wheatear stitch is a variation of a chained stitch and is a useful border stitch.

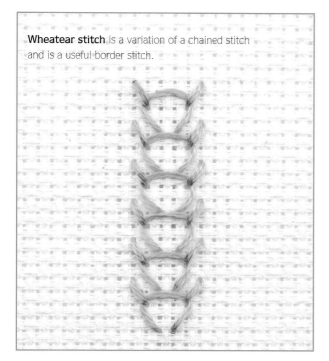

1 Bring the needle out at A. Take 2 diagonal stitches in opposite directions, from A–B and C–D, to form a V-shape with a slight gap in the middle. Come up at E, between B and D.

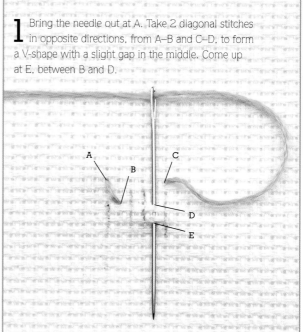

2 Slide the needle under the 2 diagonal stitches from right to left without piercing the fabric.

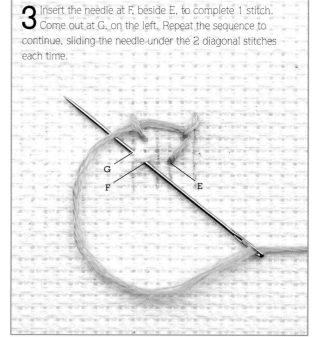

3 Insert the needle at F, beside E, to complete 1 stitch. Come out at G, on the left. Repeat the sequence to continue, sliding the needle under the 2 diagonal stitches each time.

CABLE CHAIN STITCH

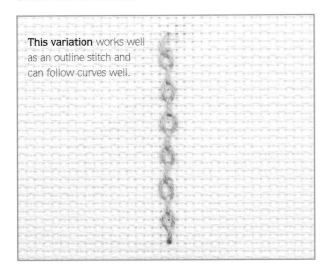

This variation works well as an outline stitch and can follow curves well.

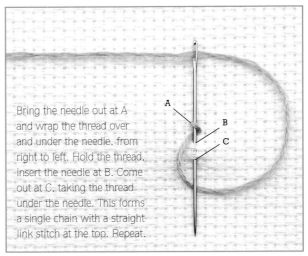

Bring the needle out at A and wrap the thread over and under the needle, from right to left. Hold the thread, insert the needle at B. Come out at C, taking the thread under the needle. This forms a single chain with a straight link stitch at the top. Repeat.

Knotted stitches

The stitches shown here all include a decorative surface knot that gives three-dimensional texture. Single knots can be scattered across a surface or tightly grouped to make a solid filling.

FRENCH KNOT

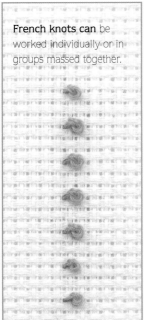

French knots can be worked individually or in groups massed together.

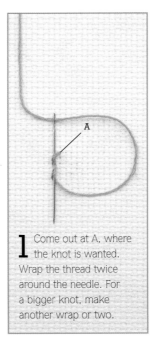

1 Come out at A, where the knot is wanted. Wrap the thread twice around the needle. For a bigger knot, make another wrap or two.

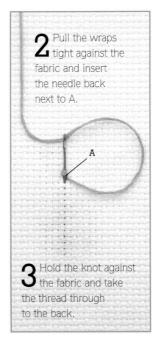

2 Pull the wraps tight against the fabric and insert the needle back next to A.

3 Hold the knot against the fabric and take the thread through to the back.

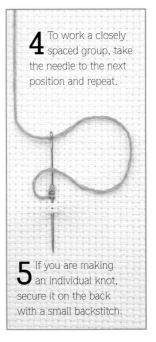

4 To work a closely spaced group, take the needle to the next position and repeat.

5 If you are making an individual knot, secure it on the back with a small backstitch.

BULLION KNOT

This long knotted stitch is best worked using a relatively thick needle with a small eye to make the coil wide enough to slide through.

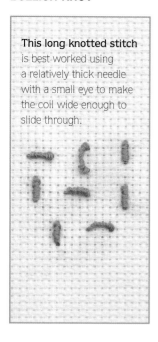

1 Come out at A and backstitch to B, without taking the stitch through.

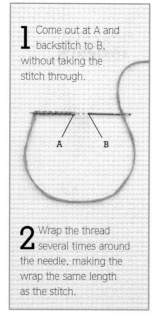

2 Wrap the thread several times around the needle, making the wrap the same length as the stitch.

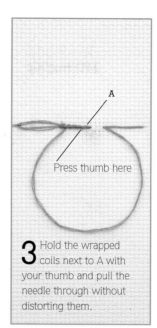

A

Press thumb here

3 Hold the wrapped coils next to A with your thumb and pull the needle through without distorting them.

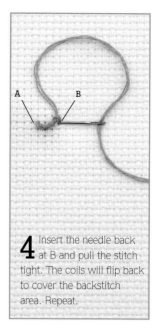

A   B

4 Insert the needle back at B and pull the stitch tight. The coils will flip back to cover the backstitch area. Repeat.

CHINESE KNOT

Also known as a forbidden knot, this stitch is smaller and flatter than a French knot.

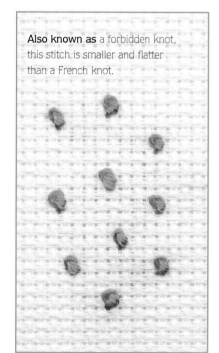

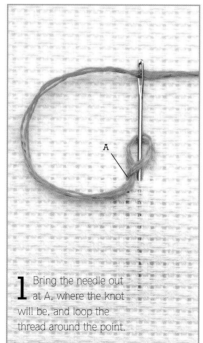

A

1 Bring the needle out at A, where the knot will be, and loop the thread around the point.

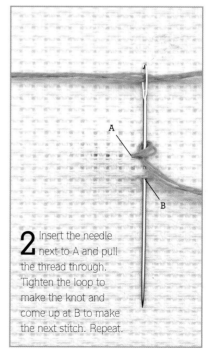

A

B

2 Insert the needle next to A and pull the thread through. Tighten the loop to make the knot and come up at B to make the next stitch. Repeat.

FOUR-LEGGED KNOT

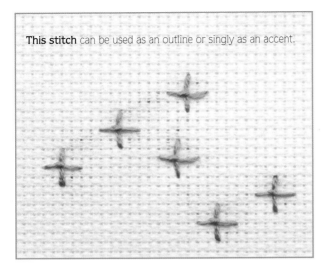

This stitch can be used as an outline or singly as an accent.

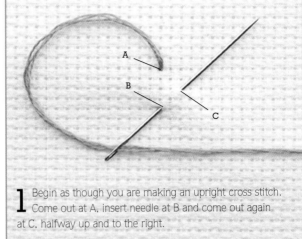

1 Begin as though you are making an upright cross stitch. Come out at A, insert needle at B and come out again at C, halfway up and to the right.

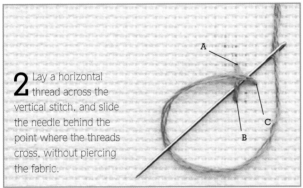

2 Lay a horizontal thread across the vertical stitch, and slide the needle behind the point where the threads cross, without piercing the fabric.

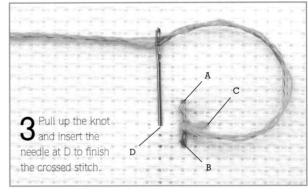

3 Pull up the knot and insert the needle at D to finish the crossed stitch.

CORAL STITCH

Coral stitch, also called knotted or beaded stitch, makes a knotted line; knots can be evenly or randomly spaced.

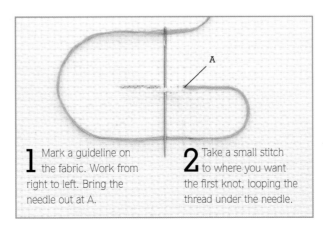

1 Mark a guideline on the fabric. Work from right to left. Bring the needle out at A.

2 Take a small stitch to where you want the first knot, looping the thread under the needle.

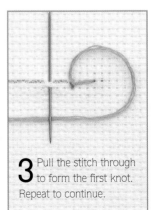

3 Pull the stitch through to form the first knot. Repeat to continue.

SCROLL STITCH

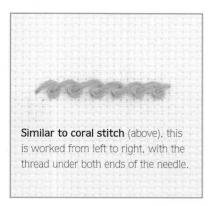

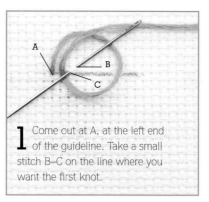

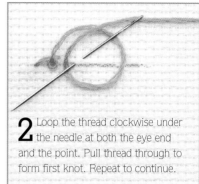

Similar to coral stitch (above), this is worked from left to right, with the thread under both ends of the needle.

1 Come out at A, at the left end of the guideline. Take a small stitch B–C on the line where you want the first knot.

2 Loop the thread clockwise under the needle at both the eye end and the point. Pull thread through to form first knot. Repeat to continue.

Couching

Couching is the name given to the technique of anchoring laid threads, which are attached to the background fabric only at the ends, with small stitches along their length. The couching is often worked in contrasting colors for a decorative effect.

COUCHING STITCH

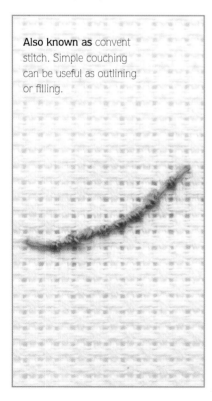

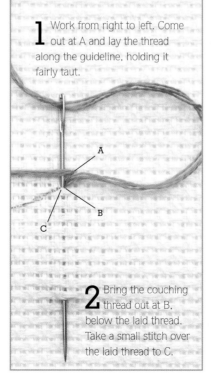

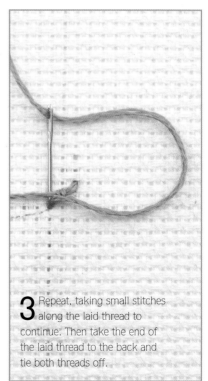

Also known as convent stitch. Simple couching can be useful as outlining or filling.

1 Work from right to left. Come out at A and lay the thread along the guideline, holding it fairly taut.

2 Bring the couching thread out at B, below the laid thread. Take a small stitch over the laid thread to C.

3 Repeat, taking small stitches along the laid thread to continue. Then take the end of the laid thread to the back and tie both threads off.

OVERCAST TRAILING

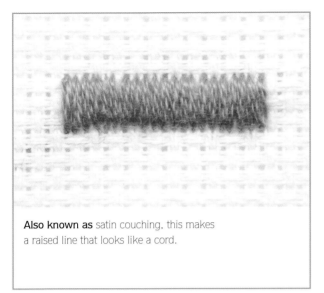

Also known as satin couching, this makes a raised line that looks like a cord.

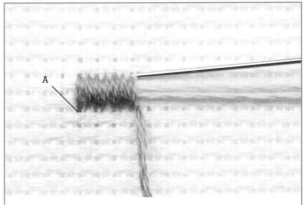

Bring the laid thread out at A and lay it along the guideline, holding it fairly taut. Bring the couching thread out at A and work small satin stitches (see page 78) next to each other over the laid threads to cover them completely.

THORN STITCH

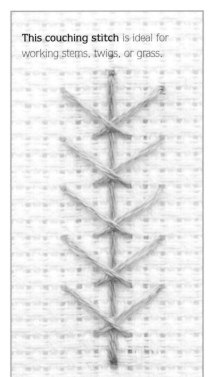

This couching stitch is ideal for working stems, twigs, or grass.

1 Come out at A, at the top. Hold the thread taut. Bring the couching thread out at B and insert at C, crossing diagonally over the laid thread.

2 Come out at D, level with B on the opposite side. Insert the needle at E, crossing diagonally over the laid thread in the opposite direction.

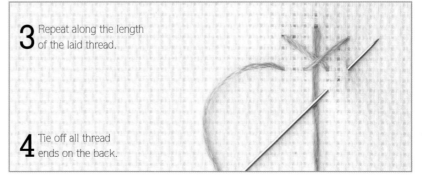

3 Repeat along the length of the laid thread.

4 Tie off all thread ends on the back.

Surface embroidery

ROUMANIAN STITCH

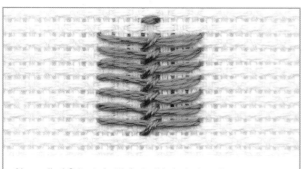

Also called Oriental stitch, in this technique the same thread is used for both the laid work and the couching. Roumanian stitch is used for borders and works well to fill leaf and flower shapes.

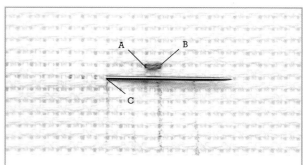

1 Mark 2 guidelines close to the center of the area to be filled. Bring the needle out at A, on the left line. Take a horizontal stitch from edge to edge, inserting the needle at B and coming out at C.

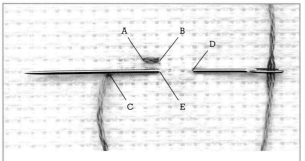

2 Take the needle across and insert it at D on the right-hand edge, coming out at E, right of center, with the needle over the working thread.

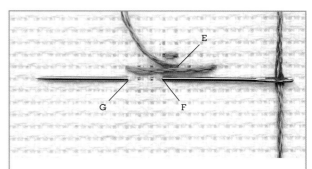

3 Take a small diagonal stitch over the horizontal one, inserting the needle at F, left of center, and coming out at G, on the edge.

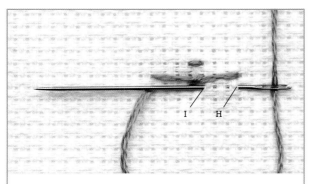

4 Make another horizontal stitch to H on the right-hand edge, coming out at I, right of center, with the needle over the working thread.

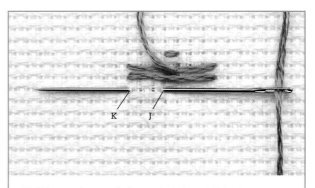

5 Take another small diagonal stitch to J, left of center, and come out at K on the left-hand edge. Repeat to continue, until the line or shape is filled.

Bokhara couching is similar to Roumanian stitch, but uses more stitches in the couching. It is suitable for filling large shapes. The couching stitches are worked over the laid thread from below.

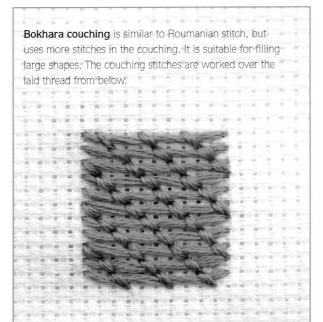

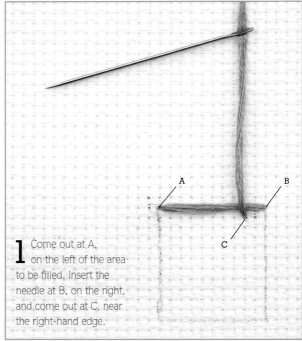

1 Come out at A, on the left of the area to be filled. Insert the needle at B, on the right, and come out at C, near the right-hand edge.

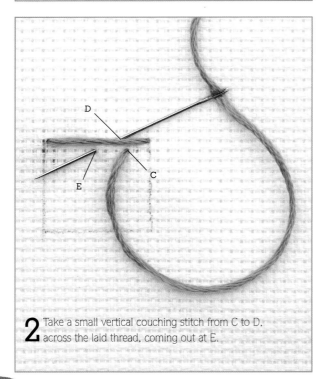

2 Take a small vertical couching stitch from C to D, across the laid thread, coming out at E.

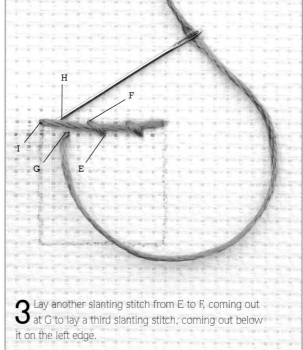

3 Lay another slanting stitch from E to F, coming out at G to lay a third slanting stitch, coming out below it on the left edge.

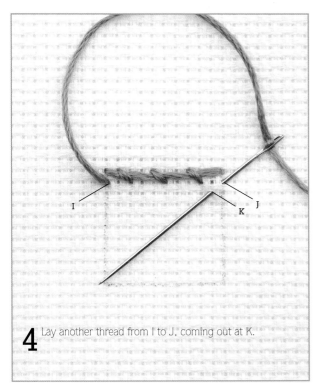

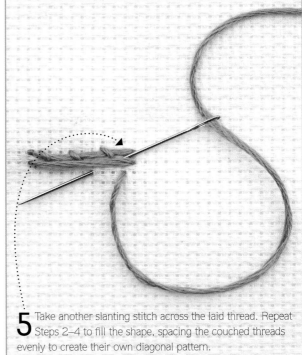

4 Lay another thread from I to J, coming out at K.

5 Take another slanting stitch across the laid thread. Repeat Steps 2–4 to fill the shape, spacing the couched threads evenly to create their own diagonal pattern.

JACOBEAN TRELLIS

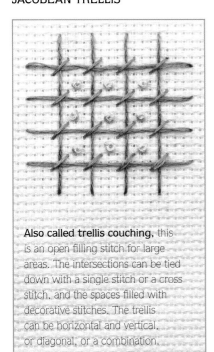

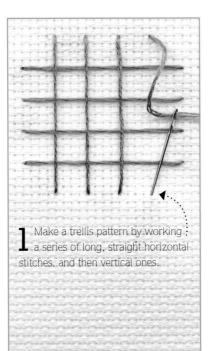

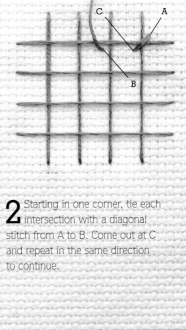

Also called trellis couching, this is an open filling stitch for large areas. The intersections can be tied down with a single stitch or a cross stitch, and the spaces filled with decorative stitches. The trellis can be horizontal and vertical, or diagonal, or a combination.

1 Make a trellis pattern by working a series of long, straight horizontal stitches, and then vertical ones.

2 Starting in one corner, tie each intersection with a diagonal stitch from A to B. Come out at C and repeat in the same direction to continue.

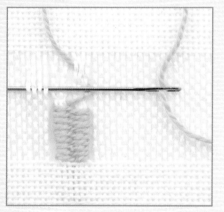 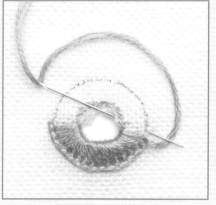 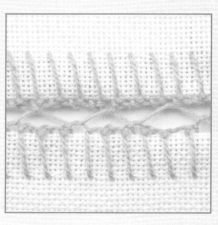

OPENWORK

Openwork

Openwork embroidery includes cutwork and broderie anglaise or eyelet work, which are known as whitework, drawn and pulled thread work, and insertion work, also known as faggoting. Each of these techniques opens up areas of the background fabric to create lacelike effects, each very different. Most of the techniques can be worked on plain- or even-weave fabric.

Whitework

Whitework includes several embroidery techniques that were used on delicate clothing and household linens that in the past were white. Whitework includes cutwork, a technique in which areas are stitched and then the background fabric is cut away. Broderie anglaise is the other main form of whitework. Delicate plain-weave fabrics, such as lawn and voile, and fine linen and cambric are suitable. Traditionally white thread is used; we have used a colored thread to show the process clearly.

OVERCAST BAR

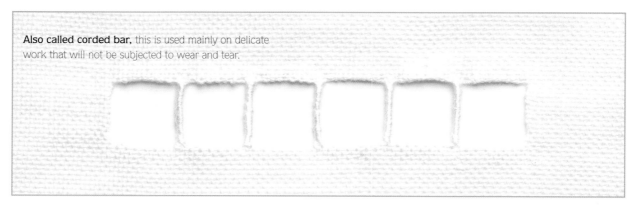

Also called corded bar, this is used mainly on delicate work that will not be subjected to wear and tear.

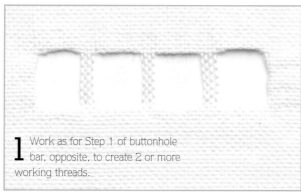

1 Work as for Step 1 of buttonhole bar, opposite, to create 2 or more working threads.

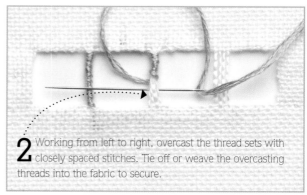

2 Working from left to right, overcast the thread sets with closely spaced stitches. Tie off or weave the overcasting threads into the fabric to secure.

BUTTONHOLE BAR

Buttonhole bars are used to connect separate pieces of fabric. You need at least 3 working threads to build on.

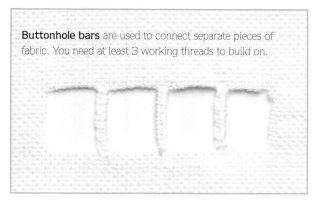

1 Even-weave fabric: withdraw vertical threads to the desired width and cut away the horizontal threads between sets of 3 threads (see page 119).

2 Plain-weave fabric: work 3 threads across the space to be filled or work running stitch across the center of the bar.

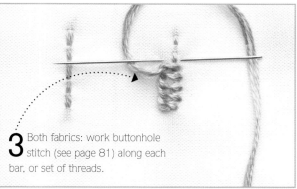

3 Both fabrics: work buttonhole stitch (see page 81) along each bar, or set of threads.

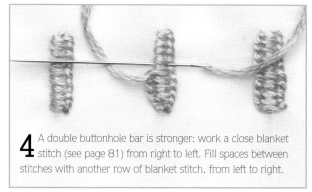

4 A double buttonhole bar is stronger: work a close blanket stitch (see page 81) from right to left. Fill spaces between stitches with another row of blanket stitch, from left to right.

WOVEN BAR

Also called needleweaving bar, this is a strong stitch that is useful on table linens.

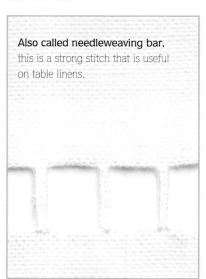

1 Work as for Step 1 of buttonhole bar, opposite, to create an even number of at least 4 working threads.

2 Come up in the center of the bar of threads. Take needle to the left, then behind the bar and back up in the center; pull the stitch tight. Take the needle to the right, behind the bar, and back up in the center; pull the stitch tight.

LOOPED EDGING

Looped edging looks similar to buttonhole stitch, but the working method is slightly different.

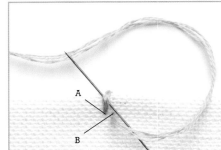

1 Press a narrow single hem. Come up at A. Slightly to the right, take a vertical stitch from back to front at B. Pull the thread through, leaving a small loop on the edge (see Step 2). Take the needle through the loop and pull gently to make a small knot on the edge.

2 Come up at C and repeat to continue.

ANTWERP EDGING

Also known as knot stitch edging, this is worked from left to right and creates a decorative lacy edging on plain-weave fabrics. Hem before beginning.

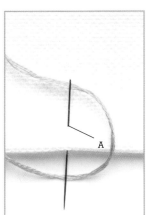

1 Insert the needle at A along stitched hemline, which acts as a guide. Come out under the edge of fabric, leaving a tail of thread on the front. Loop the thread under the needle.

2 Pull thread through, leaving a tail at the end. Slide needle behind both threads and over the working thread, below where looped threads cross. Pull knot to secure it next to the folded hem.

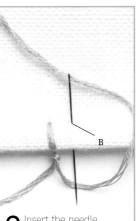

3 Insert the needle at B to continue. Darn both ends into the hem to finish.

OVERCAST EYELET

Eyelets are outlined with a variety of stitches. Overcast eyelets, which can be round or oval, are simple to work.

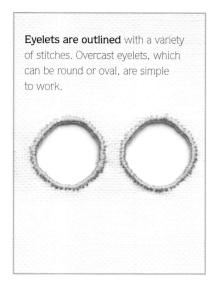

1 Mark the desired shape lightly on the fabric. Outline with small running stitches.

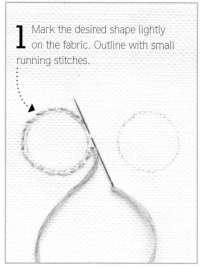

2 Cut a cross shape in the center area, but do not remove. Fold the fabric flaps to the back and overcast along the edge of the shape.

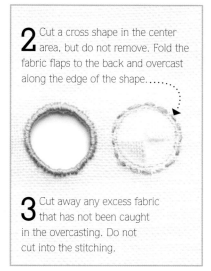

3 Cut away any excess fabric that has not been caught in the overcasting. Do not cut into the stitching.

BUTTONHOLE EYELET

Similar to overcast eyelets, buttonhole eyelets are more substantial. They can be any shape.

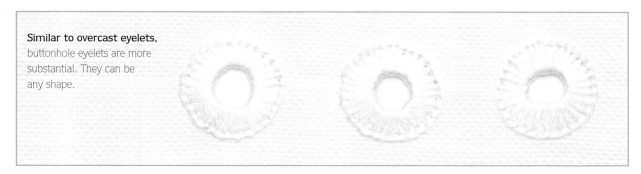

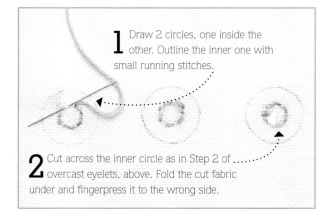

1 Draw 2 circles, one inside the other. Outline the inner one with small running stitches.

2 Cut across the inner circle as in Step 2 of overcast eyelets, above. Fold the cut fabric under and fingerpress it to the wrong side.

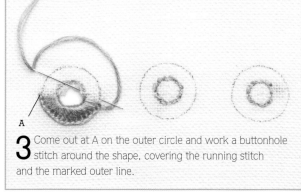

A

3 Come out at A on the outer circle and work a buttonhole stitch around the shape, covering the running stitch and the marked outer line.

SQUARE EYELET

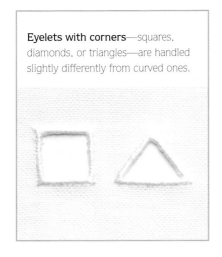

Eyelets with corners—squares, diamonds, or triangles—are handled slightly differently from curved ones.

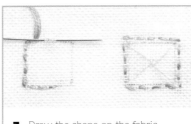

1 Draw the shape on the fabric and outline it with small running stitches. Cut diagonally across the shape into the corners and fingerpress the fabric to the wrong side.

2 Come up at A in a corner and make closely spaced overcasting stitches around the shape. Angle the stitches at the corners to make a sharp outline. To finish, weave the thread into the stitching on the wrong side and trim away excess fabric.

SOLID EDGES

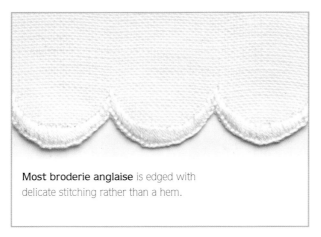

Most broderie anglaise is edged with delicate stitching rather than a hem.

1 Mark the desired pattern on the fabric and draw in both outer and inner edges as guidelines.

2 Work a foundation between the guidelines. Use a line of running stitch inside each outline, filling with rows of running stitch, or fill with chain stitch.

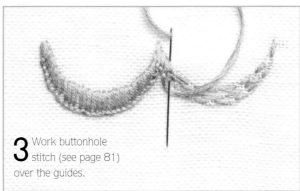

3 Work buttonhole stitch (see page 81) over the guides.

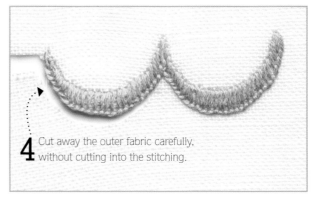

4 Cut away the outer fabric carefully, without cutting into the stitching.

LOOP PICOT

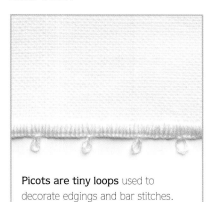

Picots are tiny loops used to decorate edgings and bar stitches. Loop picots are the easiest to work.

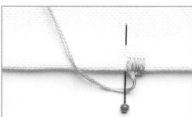

1 Working from right to left, buttonhole stitch (see page 81) along the folded edge. Where you want to add a loop, place a pin next to the last stitch you took, facing inward from the edge (so that you don't catch your finger).

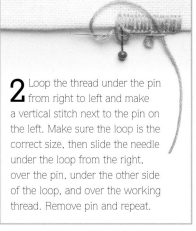

2 Loop the thread under the pin from right to left and make a vertical stitch next to the pin on the left. Make sure the loop is the correct size, then slide the needle under the loop from the right, over the pin, under the other side of the loop, and over the working thread. Remove pin and repeat.

RING PICOT

Like loop picots, Like loop picots, ring picots are added to a buttonholed edging as decoration.

1 Working from left to right, buttonhole stitch (see page 81) along the folded edge. To add a ring picot at A, move the needle back several stitches and slide it through 1 stitch at B, on the edge, to create a loop.

2 Take the needle through the loop and cover it with buttonhole stitches back to A. Repeat to continue.

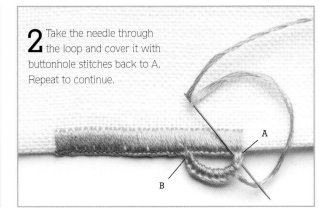

EYELET EDGES

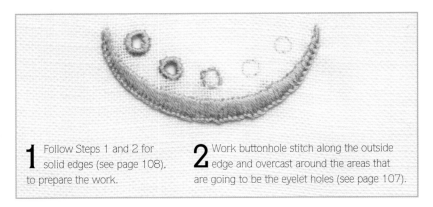

1 Follow Steps 1 and 2 for solid edges (see page 108), to prepare the work.

2 Work buttonhole stitch along the outside edge and overcast around the areas that are going to be the eyelet holes (see page 107).

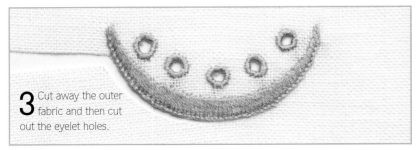

When edges incorporate eyelet holes, they are worked with a combination of buttonhole stitch and overcasting.

3 Cut away the outer fabric and then cut out the eyelet holes.

Pulled thread embroidery

This is a counted-thread embroidery technique in which threads are pulled together with tight stitches to create regular open spaces in the work. Use a tapestry needle with matching thread on soft single-thread, even-weave fabric. Work loosely in a hoop.

FOUR-SIDED STITCH

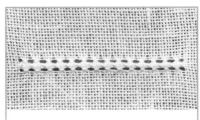

This stitch makes a lacy openwork pattern for a border or filling.

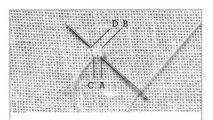

1 Come out at A. Count 4 threads up and insert needle at B. Come out at C, 4 threads down from B and 4 to the left of A. Insert needle at A again and come out at D, 4 threads up and 4 diagonally across.

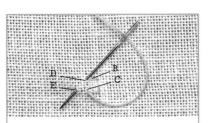

2 Insert the needle at B and come up at C. Go down at D to complete the first stitch, then come up at E, 4 down and 4 to the left of C. Repeat to make a row. To add another row, turn the work 180 degrees.

PUNCH STITCH

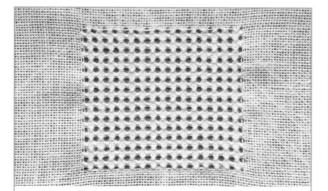

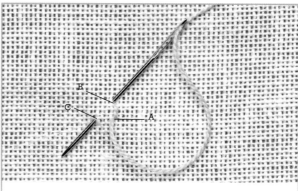

Here, double stitches worked in squares are pulled tightly to leave open spaces at each corner. Working in rows keeps the pattern regular.

1 Come out at A. Insert needle at B, 4 threads above. Come out at A again and back in at B. Come up at C, 4 threads to the left.

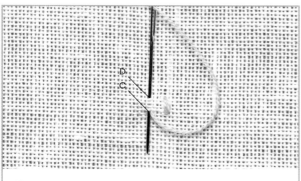

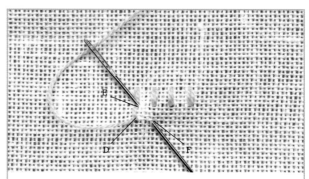

2 Work 2 vertical stitches from C to D.

3 Continue to make a row of evenly spaced upright stitches.

4 At the end of the row, come out at D, go down at E, 4 threads above. Work another double stitch, then come up at F. Work another row under the first.

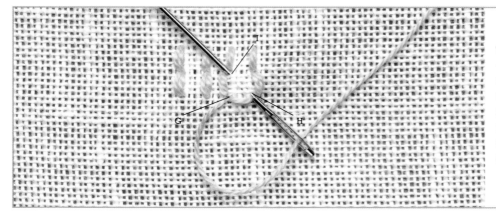

5 Come out at G. Go down at H, 4 threads to the right. Work another stitch G–H, come up at I. Continue filling in the spaces with double stitches. Pull each stitch tight.

HONEYCOMB FILLING STITCH

This light filling stitch needs to be worked tightly.

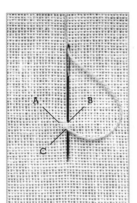

1 Come out at A. Count 3 threads to the right and insert at B. Come out at C, 3 threads below, then insert again at B and come out at C.

2 Count 3 threads to the left and insert at D. Come out 3 threads down, at E, then insert again at D and come out at E.

3 Continue back-and-forth to end of row. Turn the work 180 degrees. Repeat to create a mirror image in the next row.

STEP STITCH

This filling stitch forms a lively zigzag pattern, consisting of horizontal and vertical blocks of tightly worked straight stitches.

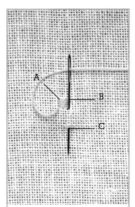

1 Come up at A and down at B, 4 threads to right. Work 4 horizontal stitches below, coming up at C, 8 threads below.

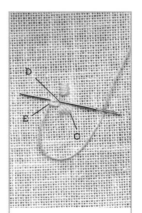

2 Work 5 vertical stitches over 4 threads, starting at C. Come up at D and down at E. Complete a block of 5 horizontal stitches.

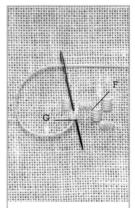

3 Work block of vertical stitches. Come up at F, work block of horizontal stitches. Come up at G to begin next block of vertical stitches.

CHESSBOARD FILLING

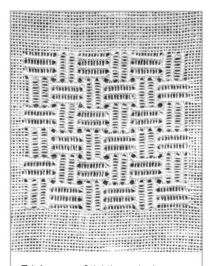

Triple rows of tightly worked alternating satin stitch (see page 78) make a solid filling with a basketweave texture.

1 Start at A, in the top left corner. Work 10 vertical straight stitches over 3 threads.

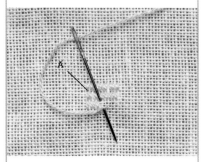

2 Reversing direction each time, repeat twice to make 2 more identical rows.

3 Come up at B and down at C, where the previous row finished. Work 10 horizontal stitches, using the holes of the previous block.

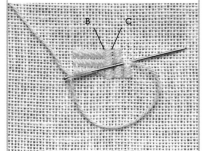

4 Reversing direction each time, repeat to make more identical rows.

WINDOW STITCH

Worked in a similar way to wave stitch (see page 115), window stitch uses a separate hole for each stitch, leaving a single thread in between.

1 Start at A, go down 4 threads and 2 to right at B. Come up at C, 5 threads to left. Insert 2 threads to right and 4 up at D. Come out at E, 5 threads to left.

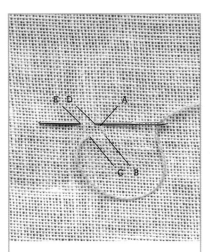

2 Repeat the sequence to complete a row, then return from left to right, reversing the diagonal stitch each time.

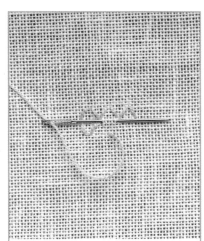

MOSAIC FILLING

Worked in groups, this gives a dense texture that has an openwork effect if the stitches are pulled tightly.

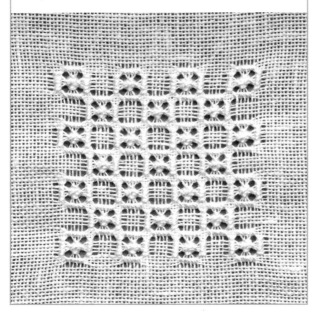

1 Start at A, work 5 vertical straight stitches over 4 threads, finishing at B.

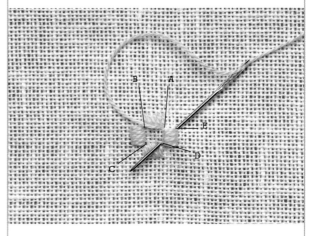

2 Work 5 horizontal stitches over 4 threads, from B to C.

3 Repeat from C to D to make 5 vertical stitches. Work 5 horizontal stitches, finishing at E.

4 From E, come out at D and work a four-sided stitch (see page 110) inside the open square, finishing at D.

5 Work a cross stitch from D to B, and then another from C to A.

6 To work subsequent stitches in a diagonal row, for a checkerboard formation, bring needle up 8 threads down and 8 to the right. Repeat the same sequence.

WAVE STITCH

This diagonal filling stitch creates a closely worked trellis effect.

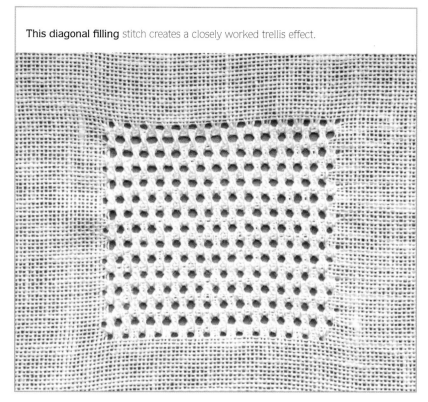

1 Come out at A, go down at B, 4 threads up and 2 to the right. Come up at C, 4 threads to the left. Insert at A and come up 4 threads to the left, at D.

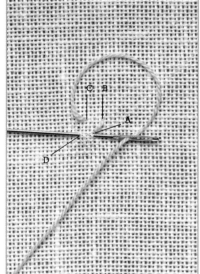

2 Insert the needle at C and come out at E. Continue in this sequence to make a row. Repeat to work subsequent rows.

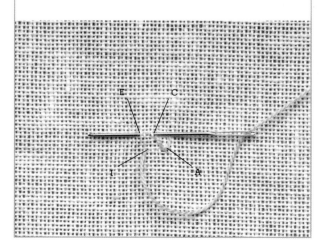

3 For the new row, go down at the top of the last stitch you made, at F, and come up at G, 8 threads below. Reinsert 4 threads above and 2 to the left at H. Work from left to right, forming a mirror image of the preceding row.

THREE-SIDED STITCH

This **stitch makes** rows of triangles with each stitch worked twice.

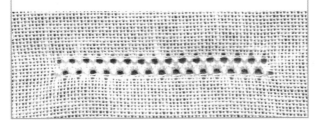

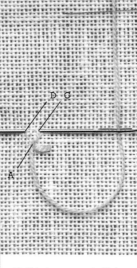

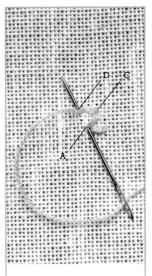

1 Come out at A and go down at B, 4 threads to the right. Work another stitch A–B. Come out at A.

2 Take the needle down at C, 2 threads to the right and 4 up. Come out at A

3 Work a second stitch A–C, coming up at D, 4 threads to the left.

4 Work 2 stitches D–C, coming up at D. Go down at A and work 2 stitches D–A. Repeat across row.

COIL FILLING

This **is simple** to work and creates a lacy openwork pattern.

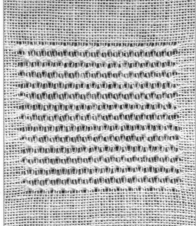

1 Come out at A and work 3 vertical satin stitches (see page 78) over 4 threads into the same hole

2 Move to B, 4 threads to the right, and repeat. Repeat sequence to finish a row.

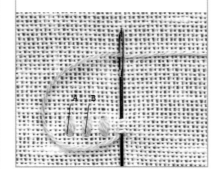

3 Begin second row at C, 4 threads down and 2 to right, repeating sequence. Make as many alternating rows as desired, pulling the thread tight.

DIAGONAL RAISED BAND

This stitch creates an open texture. It is worked in rows of upright crosses.

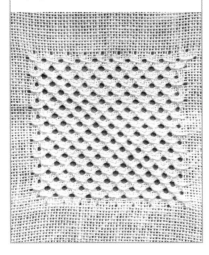

1 Come out at A and insert the needle at B, 6 threads above A. Come out at C, 3 threads to the left and 3 above A.

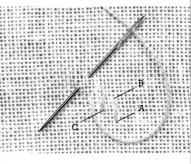

2 Continue the sequence to make a row of stepped vertical stitches.

3 Begin the second row at D, 4 threads down and 2 to left, making horizontal stitches. Make as many rows as desired, pulling the thread tight.

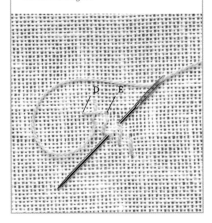

DIAMOND FILLING

Diamond filling consists of lines of staggered straight stitches. To form a diamond shape, work a row below or above the first, in mirror image.

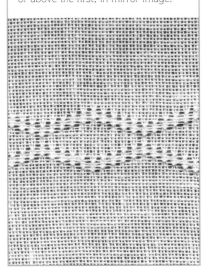

1 Come out at A and take a backstitch over 3 threads to right, to B. Come out at C, 3 threads below A, and repeat. Come out at D, 1 thread below previous top stitch, and repeat the sequence.

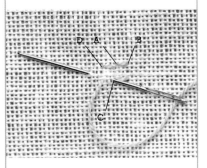

2 Repeat, making pairs of backstitches and dropping each pair 1 thread lower than previous pair.

3 After working 6 descending pairs of stitches, come up at E, 1 thread above last upper stitch. Continue to work pairs of stitches, placing them 1 thread above preceding pair.

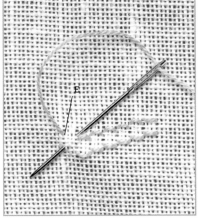

Also known as star eyelet, this can be used singly or as a checkerboard filling, with eyelets positioned so that corner stitches share holes.

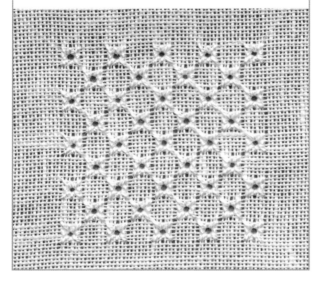

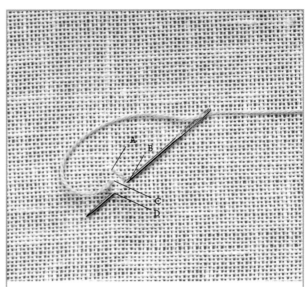

1 Start at A. Go down 3 threads and 3 to right at B. Come up at C, 3 threads to left. Insert at B again. Come up 3 threads down and 3 to left at D.

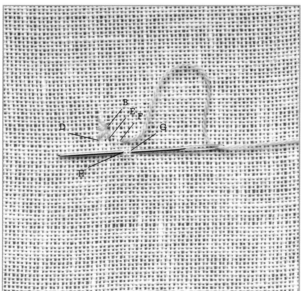

2 Come up at E, 3 threads to right of D. Reinsert at B. Come up at F, 3 threads to right of E, go down at G, the center of the next eyelet, and up at H.

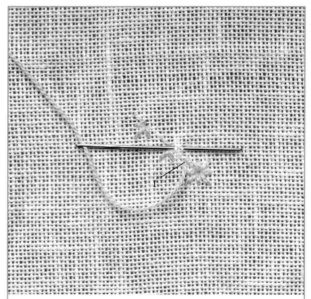

3 Repeat Steps 1–2 to make another half-eyelet. On lowest eyelet, continue around center to make 8 stitches. Come up at I to complete the next eyelet.

Drawn thread work

These techniques are used to decorate hems and create borders. They must be worked on evenweave fabrics from which individual threads are withdrawn, leaving a "ladder" of threads. Finish removed threads to prevent fraying.

REMOVING THREADS

1 Mark the area to be removed with pins. Cut a single horizontal thread in the center, leaving the vertical threads in place.

2 Carefully unpick it from the center to each end, but do not remove it completely.

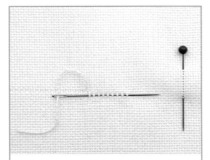

3 Thread each unpicked thread in turn onto a tapestry needle and weave it in and out beside the next thread to hide it. This will secure it so that it doesn't unravel.

TURNING A HEM

After removing the threads, turn under a double hem up to the edge of the drawn threads. Pin and then baste in place. The embroidery will hold it secure. Remove the basting when the decorative stitching is complete.

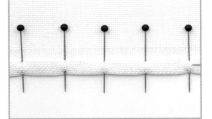

HEMSTITCH

Also known as single hemstitch, this stitch is the simplest of a group of decorative techniques for finishing hems. Work on the right side.

1 Remove the required number of threads, usually 2 or 3. Baste a hem to the lower edge of the withdrawn threads.

2 Come out at A, 2 threads below edge, picking up the top edge of hem. Slide needle under 3 to 4 threads, from B to C.

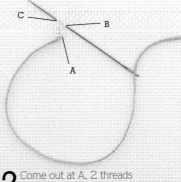

3 Pull thread through. Reinsert needle at B and come up at D, 2 threads below edge, picking up top edge of hem so that the working thread is looped around the vertical threads.

4 Pull loop tight. Repeat.

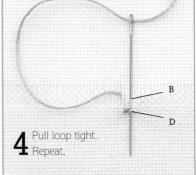

ANTIQUE HEMSTITCH

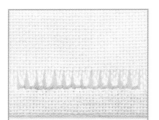

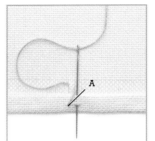

Antique hemstitch is worked like hemstitch, but from the wrong side.

Prepare the fabric. With wrong side facing, hide end of working thread and come out at A. Work as for hemstitch (see page 119)—the right side shows only a small stitch.

LADDER HEMSTITCH

Ladder hemstitch, or ladder stitch, is worked on both sides of the row of withdrawn thread. Ladder stitch can also be worked in the same way as antique hemstitch.

Prepare the fabric. Work as in Step 1 of hemstitch. At the end of the bottom row, turn the work upside down. Still with right side facing, work a row along the top. The stitching must match the groups of threads on the first row.

ZIGZAG HEMSTITCH

Also called serpentine or trellis hemstitch, this variation on ladder hemstitch creates a zigzag pattern.

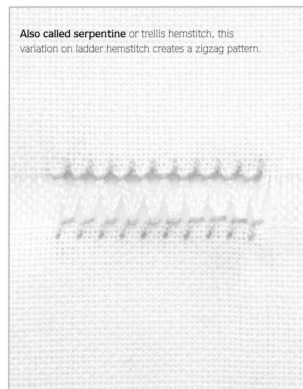

1 Prepare the fabric. Work hemstitch along lower edge of drawn threads. Ensure an even number of threads in each group.

2 Turn work upside down. Work row of hemstitch along top edge, sliding the needle under the center 2 threads, to create a zigzag.

INTERLACED HEMSTITCH

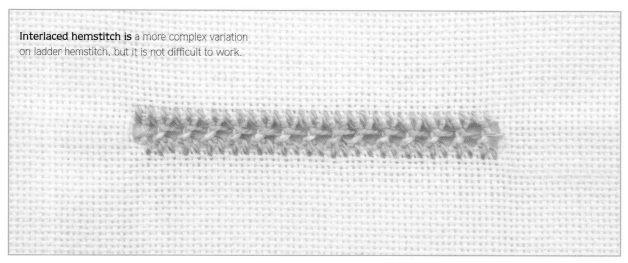

Interlaced hemstitch is a more complex variation on ladder hemstitch, but it is not difficult to work.

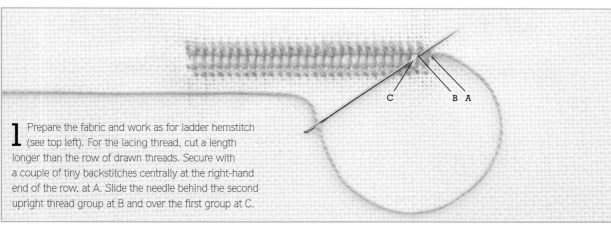

C   B A

1 Prepare the fabric and work as for ladder hemstitch (see top left). For the lacing thread, cut a length longer than the row of drawn threads. Secure with a couple of tiny backstitches centrally at the right-hand end of the row, at A. Slide the needle behind the second upright thread group at B and over the first group at C.

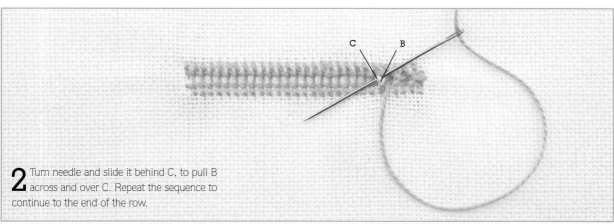

C   B

2 Turn needle and slide it behind C, to pull B across and over C. Repeat the sequence to continue to the end of the row.

DIAMOND HEMSTITCH

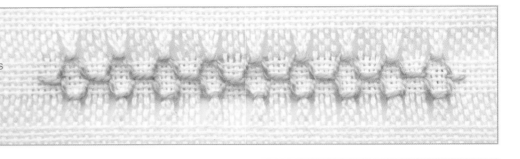

Also called diamond border, this variation is worked along two rows of withdrawn threads and over the band of remaining threads between them.

1 Prepare the fabric, but withdraw threads from 2 parallel rows, leaving an undisturbed row with an even number of threads in between.

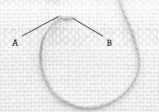

2 Come out at A, in the center of the uncut row. Insert at B, 4 threads to the right. Slide needle back to A behind the thread group. Pull tightly.

3 Insert the needle at C, at the base of the top drawn-thread row. Come out at D, 4 threads to the left. Slide needle from C to D. Pull stitch tightly.

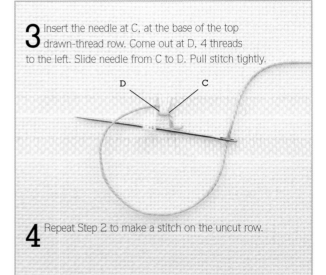

4 Repeat Step 2 to make a stitch on the uncut row.

5 Insert the needle at E, behind the next group of threads in the withdrawn row. Come out at F. Repeat Steps 2–5 to continue.

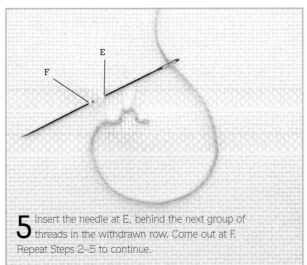

6 At the end of the row, turn the work upside down and work the second row in the same way, using the same holes as before in the center row.

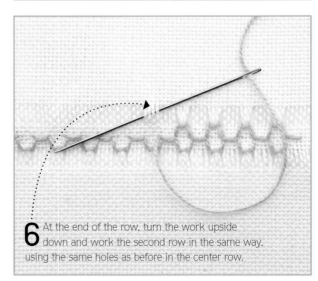

WOVEN HEMSTITCH

Woven hemstitch, also called needleweaving, is similar to a woven bar (see page 105).

1 Prepare the fabric as in Step 1 of hemstitch (see page 119), removing 4 or 5 threads. Come out at A. Insert at B, 4 threads to the right. Come out at A. Insert at C, 4 threads to the left, and come out again above A.

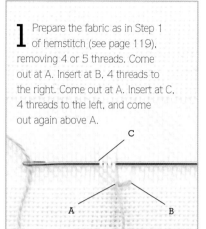

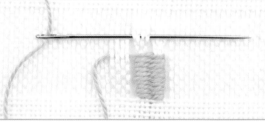

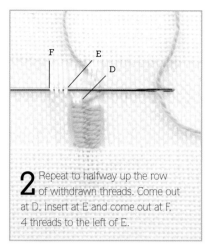

2 Repeat to halfway up the row of withdrawn threads. Come out at D, insert at E and come out at F, 4 threads to the left of E.

3 Bring the needle out on the left-hand edge, insert in the center of the row, and come out again 4 threads to the right and work to the top of the withdrawn threads.

4 Turn the work upside down. Insert the needle on the right of the new row. Weave as before. To finish, slide the needle under a row of stitches on the wrong side.

Insertions

Insertions, also called faggoting, are decorative stitches that hold two pieces of fabric together in an openwork seam. The technique developed from a need to join the narrow widths of fabric woven on early looms to make household textiles, and it adds a pretty effect to table and bed linens.

MOUNTING THE FABRIC

To begin, both fabrics should be hemmed along the edges to be joined. Draw parallel lines ¼in (5mm) apart on a strip of stiff paper, line up the edges of the fabric along them, and baste to stabilize the surface and keep the stitches even.

Basting stitches

BUTTONHOLE INSERTION STITCH

Buttonhole insertion is a strong faggot stitch that can also be used on plain-weave fabric. You can make more stitches in each group or vary the number. Use at least three per group for strength and stability.

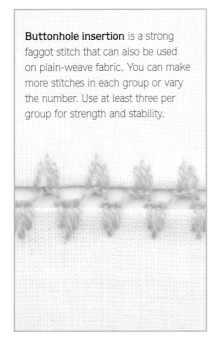

1 Mount on paper (see page 123). Work a buttonhole stitch (see page 81) on one edge from A to B. Work a set of 3 stitches along the top edge. Insert needle at C on the lower edge, with needle over the working thread.

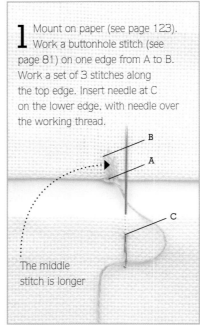

The middle stitch is longer

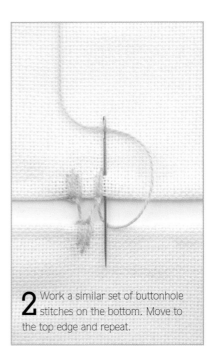

2 Work a similar set of buttonhole stitches on the bottom. Move to the top edge and repeat.

KNOTTED INSERTION STITCH

This stitch makes a textured insertion suitable for a narrow join.

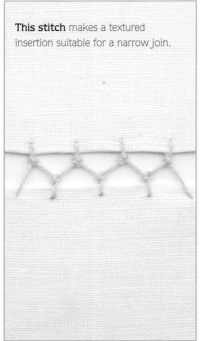

1 Mount on paper. Secure the working thread and take a diagonal stitch from the bottom edge to the top. Come out on the wrong side at A.

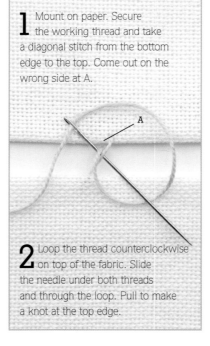

2 Loop the thread counterclockwise on top of the fabric. Slide the needle under both threads and through the loop. Pull to make a knot at the top edge.

3 Take a diagonal stitch to the lower edge, coming out on the wrong side at B. Loop the thread clockwise. Slide the needle under both threads and through the loop. Pull to make a knot.

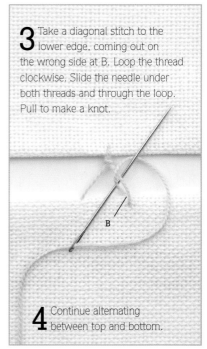

4 Continue alternating between top and bottom.

TWISTED INSERTION STITCH

Also known as faggoting, twisted insertion stitch is a quick way of making a pretty openwork join.

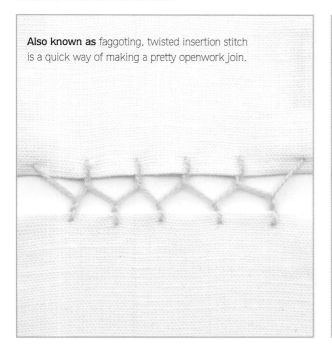

1 Mount on paper. Secure the working thread on the left side of the top edge. Take a diagonal stitch to the lower edge. Bring the needle out at A, on the right side.

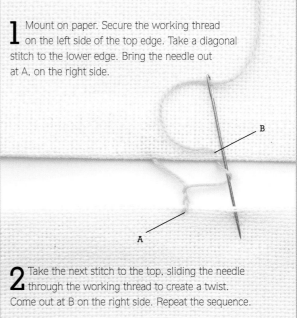

2 Take the next stitch to the top, sliding the needle through the working thread to create a twist. Come out at B on the right side. Repeat the sequence.

LACED INSERTION STITCH

This stitch depends on the lacing thread for its strength, so choose carefully and keep the tension equal.

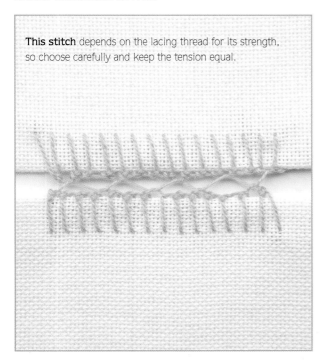

1 Work a row of Antwerp edging (see page 106) or knotted buttonhole edging along each edge. Mount on paper. Come out at A, through a loop on the lower edging.

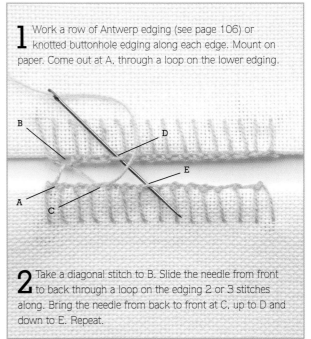

2 Take a diagonal stitch to B. Slide the needle from front to back through a loop on the edging 2 or 3 stitches along. Bring the needle from back to front at C, up to D and down to E. Repeat.

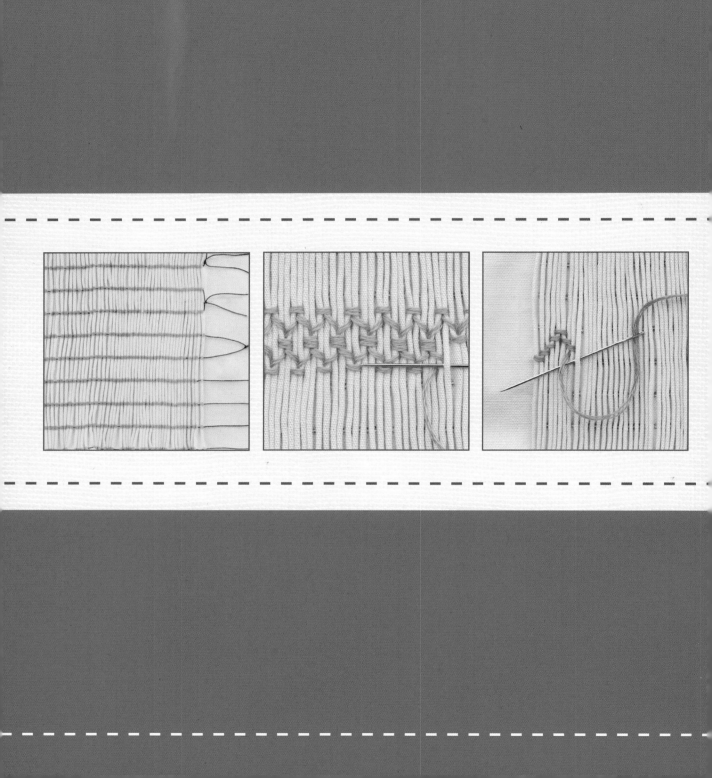

SMOCKING

Smocking

Smocking has traditionally been used to decorate the gathers in the bodices of dresses, blouses, christening robes, and, of course, smocks. Because the gathers add depth and weight to the finished garment, it is recommended to use a lightweight, closely woven fabric such as cotton or silk. Stranded cotton thread is best, traditionally in a color to match the fabric, but contrasting colored threads can create wonderful effects.

Smocking basics

Many basic embroidery stitches can be worked over the gathers, alone or in combination. Remember that smocking takes more fabric, usually about three times the desired finished width. Fabrics with even checks, such as gingham and dotted patterns, can be used, since they provide built-in guidelines. The gathering thread should be strong, but the color doesn't matter, since the thread will be removed.

MARKING THE GATHERS

1 Mark the fabric to make sure that the gathers are even. To mark by hand, measure vertical lines to delineate the spaces between folds in the gathers and then mark horizontal threads with a dot to create stitching lines.

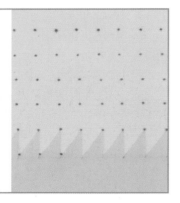

2 It is quicker, however, to use a printed transfer that has evenly spaced dots that can be ironed onto the wrong side of the fabric. Make sure there are an even number of horizontal rows.

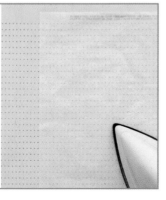

STITCHING THE GATHERS

1 To stitch the gathers, cut a length of thread long enough to finish a row with thread left over and knot it securely.

2 Take a small stitch at each marked dot, but do not pull the thread tight. Use a new thread for each marked row.

3 Pull the loose ends of the threads gently, 1 row at a time, until the piece measures the correct width.

4 Tie the loose ends in pairs and, working from the right side, even up the gathers.

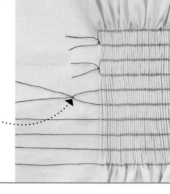

ROPE STITCH

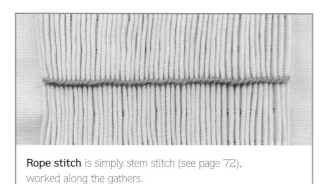

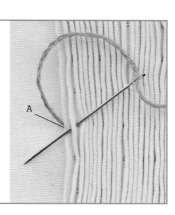

Rope stitch is simply stem stitch (see page 72), worked along the gathers.

Bring the needle out at A, on the left-hand fold, and work stem stitch in a straight line, picking up the top of each gather. Keep the thread consistently either above or below the needle.

CABLE STITCH

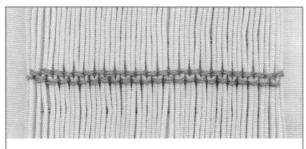

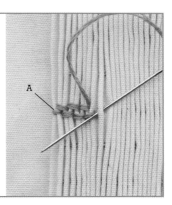

Cable stitch is stronger than rope stitch and holds the gathers firmly.

Bring the needle out at A as for rope stitch, above. Work stem stitch in a straight line, picking up the top of each gather, but alternating the position of the thread (above and then below the needle) with each stitch.

VANDYKE STITCH

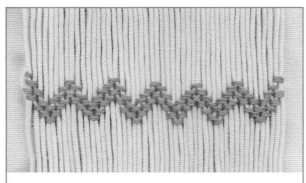

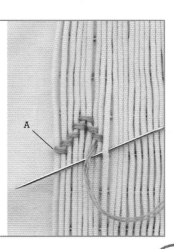

Vandyke stitch is another, more decorative, smocking stitch based on stem stitch.

1 Bring the needle out at A as for rope stitch, above, and work stem stitch in a chevron pattern.

2 Keep the thread below the needle to work in an upward line and above the needle to work down.

Honeycomb smocking

Honeycomb stitch (see page 112) can be stitched with the working thread on either side of the fabric. The effect from the front is very different from that of the back.

CLOSED HONEYCOMB STITCH

Closed honeycomb stitch is worked with the thread on the right side of the work.

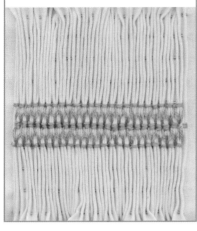

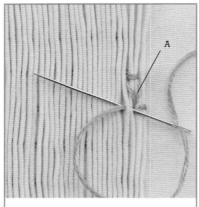

1 Come out at A, on the second fold of the second row. Backstitch through the first 2 folds. On the first row, backstitch through folds 2 and 3. Repeat.

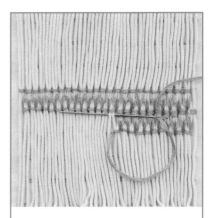

2 On the next row of stitching, work backstitches along the third row, but simply slide the needle under the backstitches on row 2.

OPEN HONEYCOMB STITCH

Open honeycomb stitch is worked with the thread on the wrong side of the work.

1 Bring the needle out at A and take a horizontal backstitch through the first 2 folds, working from left to right.

2 Bring the needle out at the second fold on row 2 and make a backstitch that pulls folds 2 and 3 together.

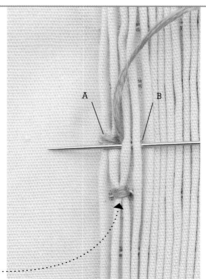

3 Go back to the first row, go in at B, and come out at the third fold.

4 Backstitch to pull folds 3 and 4 together. Repeat the sequence to finish the row. Work subsequent rows the same way.

HONEYCOMB CHEVRON STITCH

Honeycomb chevron is a stitch often found on traditional smocks. Work it from left to right, on the right side.

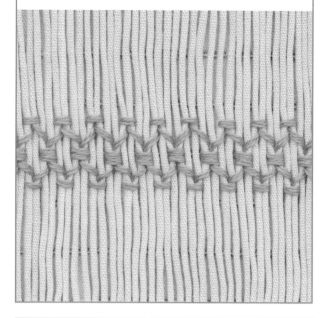

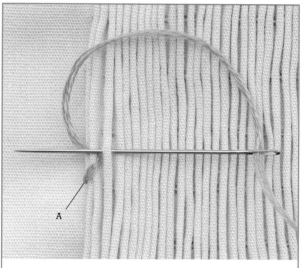

1 Bring the needle out at A on the first fold on the second row. Take it up to the first row to the right and into the second fold. Backstitch over the second and third folds and come out between them, keeping the thread below the needle.

2 Go down to the second row again to the right and insert the needle at B into the fourth fold. Backstitch over folds 4 and 5 and come out between them, with the thread above the needle.

3 Continue the sequence, alternating up and down to the end of the row.

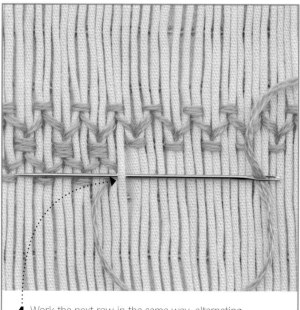

4 Work the next row in the same way, alternating the ups and downs to make a diamond pattern.

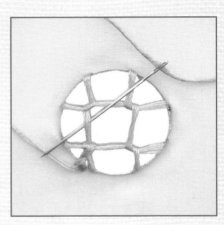

BEADWORK

Beadwork

Beads have been used to decorate textiles throughout history and in virtually every civilization in the world. Beadwork as an embroidery technique includes beads of an astonishing variety, sequins, and shisha mirrors, all of which are held on a fabric ground by stitching. The variety provides an excellent way to embellish everything from sachets and home goods to quilts, clothing, and accessories.

Beads

Beads can be used as accents or applied in rows in several ways. It is best to use a beading needle, which is thin enough to pass through almost any bead, and a polyester thread. Invisible nylon thread is ideal on plain-weave fabrics; alternatively, you can choose a thread that matches either the beads or the fabric.

SINGLE BEAD

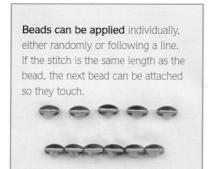

Beads can be applied individually, either randomly or following a line. If the stitch is the same length as the bead, the next bead can be attached so they touch.

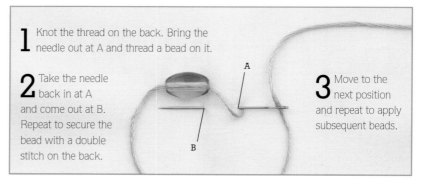

1 Knot the thread on the back. Bring the needle out at A and thread a bead on it.

2 Take the needle back in at A and come out at B. Repeat to secure the bead with a double stitch on the back.

3 Move to the next position and repeat to apply subsequent beads.

COUCHING

Couching beads is similar to couching threads (see page 97). Cut lengths of thread that are longer than the line to be covered.

1 Knot the thread on the back and bring the needle out at A.

2 Thread on the required number of beads.

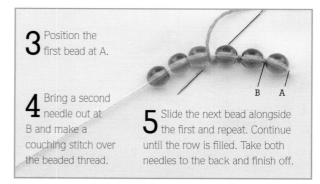

3 Position the first bead at A.

4 Bring a second needle out at B and make a couching stitch over the beaded thread.

5 Slide the next bead alongside the first and repeat. Continue until the row is filled. Take both needles to the back and finish off.

SPOT STITCH

Spot stitch is another couching technique in which several beads are grouped between each couching stitch. It is quicker to work than individual couching, but it is also less secure.

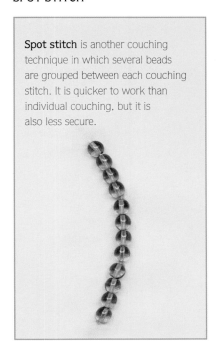

1 Work as for step 1 of couching, then slide 3 or 4 beads down to A.

2 Bring a second needle out at B and couch over the thread holding the first group of beads.

3 Slide 3 or 4 more beads down to B and couch the beaded thread at C.

4 Continue until the row or line is filled, then take both needles to the back and finish both threads off securely.

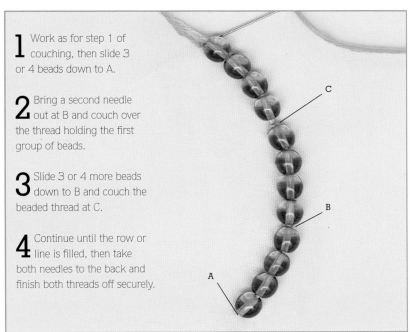

LAZY SQUAW FILLING

This is a quick method for filling an area with beads. Work in a hoop.

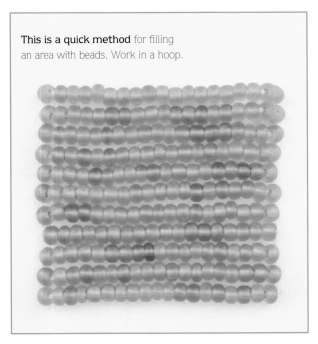

1 Mark guidelines on the area to be filled if necessary.

2 Cut a length of thread and knot it on the back.

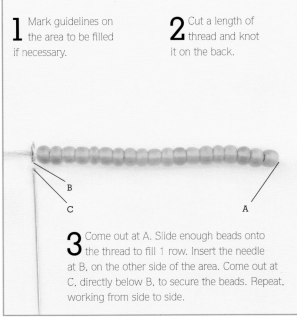

3 Come out at A. Slide enough beads onto the thread to fill 1 row. Insert the needle at B, on the other side of the area. Come out at C, directly below B, to secure the beads. Repeat, working from side to side.

OJIBWA FILLING

This is a very secure way of beading.
Outline the area to be filled with basting, which
will be covered by the beads. Work in a hoop.

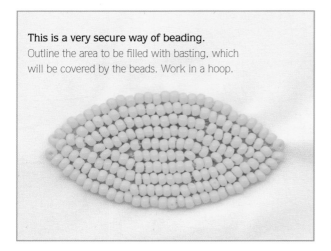

1 Knot the thread on the back.
Come out at A, on the edge.
Thread on 1 bead and apply as
for a single bead (see page 134).

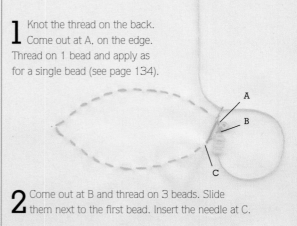

2 Come out at B and thread on 3 beads. Slide
them next to the first bead. Insert the needle at C.

3 Take a stitch back to D, coming out between the first
and second beads of group of 3. Insert the needle
at E, through the second and third beads in the group.

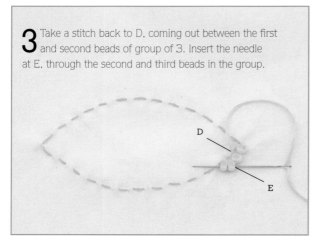

4 Add another 3 beads.
Repeat to fill the shape
from the outside in.

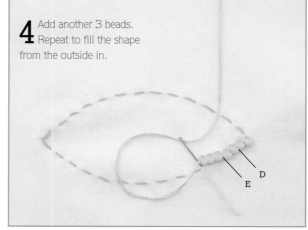

BEADED FRINGE

Use a strong thread
that is thin enough to
go through the holes
in the beads.

1 Knot the end of
the thread. Slide the
required number of beads
onto the thread.

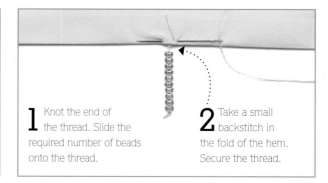

2 Take a small
backstitch in
the fold of the hem.
Secure the thread.

LOOP FRINGE

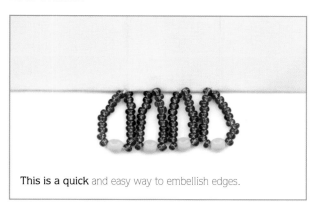

This is a quick and easy way to embellish edges.

1 Hide the knot in the hem. Bring the needle out at A. Slide the required number of beads onto the thread.

2 Insert the needle back in to A to create a loop. Come out again at B to the left. Repeat.

Sequins

A sequin is a small disk of metal or plastic with a hole in the center through which it can be attached to fabric. Traditionally, sequins are round, but they are available in a myriad of shapes and colors. They can be attached individually, in groups, or rows.

SINGLE SEQUIN

Single sequins can be attached on one or more sides. Sequins can be placed edge to edge or scattered across the surface.

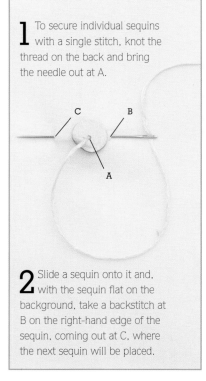

1 To secure individual sequins with a single stitch, knot the thread on the back and bring the needle out at A.

2 Slide a sequin onto it and, with the sequin flat on the background, take a backstitch at B on the right-hand edge of the sequin, coming out at C, where the next sequin will be placed.

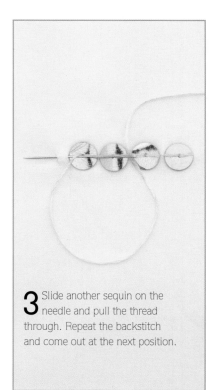

3 Slide another sequin on the needle and pull the thread through. Repeat the backstitch and come out at the next position.

SEQUIN CHAIN

An overlapping chain of sequins can be worked to create many interesting effects.

1 Knot the thread on the back and bring the needle out at A.

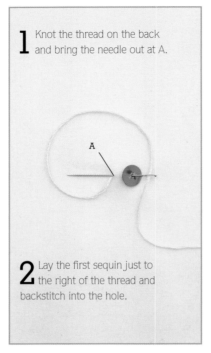

2 Lay the first sequin just to the right of the thread and backstitch into the hole.

3 Come out again at A. Slide the second sequin onto the needle.

4 Backstitch into the hole of the first sequin and come out on the left-hand edge of the second sequin. Repeat to complete the chain. Secure the thread on the back.

BEADED SEQUIN

Sequins can also be anchored to the fabric by a bead.

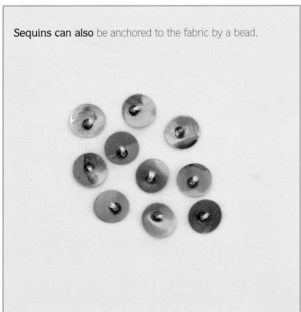

1 Lay a sequin in position and bring the needle out through the hole.

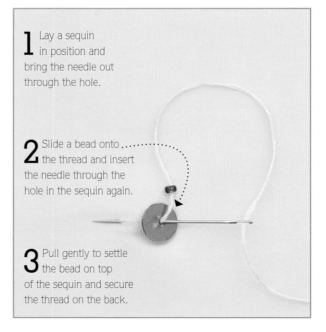

2 Slide a bead onto the thread and insert the needle through the hole in the sequin again.

3 Pull gently to settle the bead on top of the sequin and secure the thread on the back.

Mirrorwork

Also called shisha work, mirrorwork is a traditional form of textile decoration from Central Asia. Shisha are small disks of mirror, glass, or tin that are held in place by a foundation framework on which a decorative edge is stitched. On plain-weave fabrics, use a crewel needle and a single-ply thread or double-stranded floss with enough body to hold the disk securely and give a firm edge.

SINGLE THREAD METHOD

This traditional shisha stitch shows off the mirrored surface well.

1 Hold the disk in place. Bring the needle out at A.

2 Insert the needle at B and come out at C. Insert at D to make 2 parallel stitches.

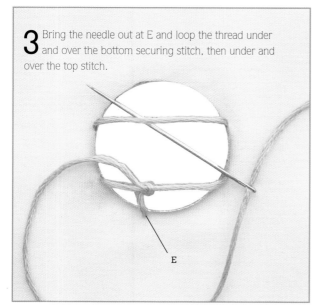

3 Bring the needle out at E and loop the thread under and over the bottom securing stitch, then under and over the top stitch.

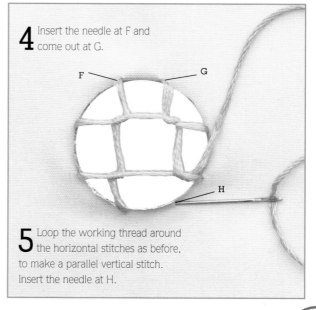

4 Insert the needle at F and come out at G.

5 Loop the working thread around the horizontal stitches as before, to make a parallel vertical stitch. Insert the needle at H.

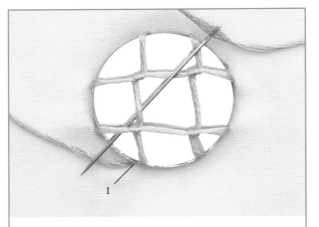

6 Bring the needle out at I and slide the needle under the crossed threads in the bottom-left corner, keeping the thread left of the needle.

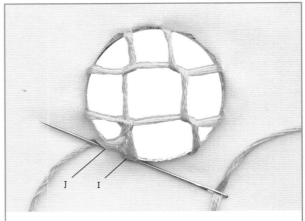

7 Insert the needle at I again and come out at J, with the needle on top of the working thread.

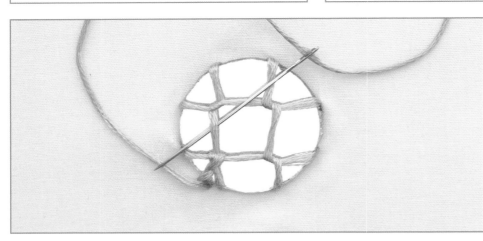

8 Slide the needle under the left-hand vertical thread and over the working thread.

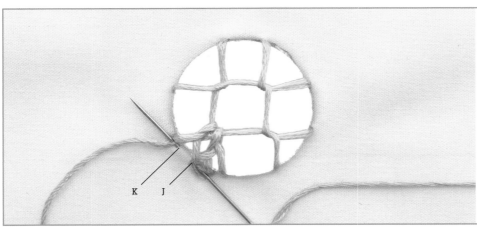

9 Insert the needle at J and come out at K, with the needle on top of the working thread.

10 Repeat the sequence of taking a small stitch through the fabric and a loop under the foundation threads to create a decorative edge.

DOUBLE THREAD METHOD

The mirror is held in place by a "frame" of 4 pairs of straight stitches. To keep the disk securely in place, work all the stitches as tightly against the edge of the mirror as possible, inserting the needle vertically against the edge each time.

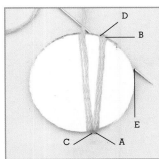

1 Hold the disk in place. Bring the needle out at A. Insert it at B and come out at C, next to A. Insert it at D, next to B, and come out at E.

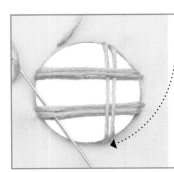

2 Repeat, making pairs of threads on all 4 sides. Each pair should cross on top of the previous pair; take the final pair under the first pair of threads.

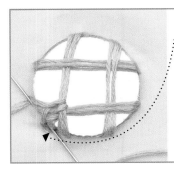

3 Working as close to the edge as possible, repeat Steps 4–7 of single thread (see pages 139–140). If you prefer, you can work a simple buttonhole stitch (see page 81).

LATTICE

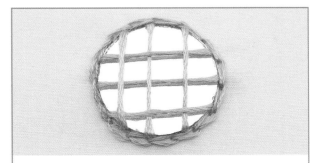

This is a simple, nontraditional mirrorwork method. Make sure that the edges of the disk are smooth so they don't cut into the thread.

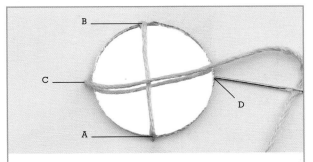

1 Work a lattice of at least 3 threads. Holding the disk in place, bring the needle out at A and take it across to B. Then take a stitch horizontally across the center from C to D. Add a stitch in each direction on either side, alternating sides as you work.

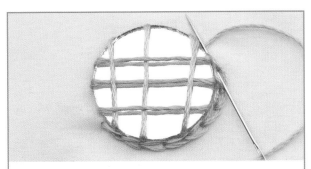

2 Add lattice threads as desired, then outline the disk with chain stitch or one of its variations (see pages 90–91), worked as close as possible to the edge.

NEEDLEPOINT DESIGNS

Needlepoint designs

Deciding what to stitch can be an exhilarating, but also sometimes bewildering, experience. There is such a wealth of commercially produced designs, as well as a wealth of needlepoint stitches tempting you to create your own designs. Here are some of the options. The key stitches and techniques of needlepoint, popular for making hard-wearing household and personal accessories, from eyeglass cases to chair seats, as well as purely decorative items such as pictures.

Ready-made designs

You can find many needlepoint designs ready for you to stitch—either in the form of a kit (with materials included), a printed canvas, or given in a book in chart form. These have one obvious advantage: all the design decisions have been made for you by a professional; all you need to do is the stitching and the making up of the project. The better-quality kits contain good materials. However, they usually include only enough yarn for the half-cross version of tent stitch (see page 162), so if you want to use a different form of tent stitch, you will have to buy extra yarn.

TYPES OF READY-MADE DESIGNS

Kits: A needlepoint kit usually consists of a canvas with the design printed on it in colors approximating those of the yarns, the yarns themselves, and a tapestry needle. If the design is to be worked in half-cross stitch, this should be stated in the instructions. If so, make sure that the canvas is either double or interlock (see page 152). Otherwise, there is a risk of stitches slipping between intersecting canvas threads. Or you could work the design in a different form of tent stitch. You will need to buy more thread for those stitches (see page 152). If the kit does not state the brand of thread used, you will need to contact the manufacturer for this information.

Printed canvases: These designs consist only of a printed canvas, with a color key designating the recommended shades of a certain brand of yarn. Their main advantage, relative to a kit, is that you can choose your own yarn (useful if that brand is not easily available) and, if you like, buy it in stages. You will need to amend the color key, of course. If you intend to work the design in half-cross stitch, make sure the canvas is of interlock or double-thread construction.

Partially worked canvases: On some canvases a central motif has been completed—or marked with tramé (see page 163). The purchaser then works just the background (or, in the latter case, also the tent stitches over the tramé). Some traméed canvases are very complex and challenging. However, if you choose one that includes a large background of solid-colored tent stitch, you may find the work rather boring. Consider working the background in a larger, more textured stitch, such as gobelin filling (page 174), encroaching gobelin (page 165), or long stitch (page 177). The work will be finished more quickly and you will have given it your own creative stamp.

CHARTED DESIGNS

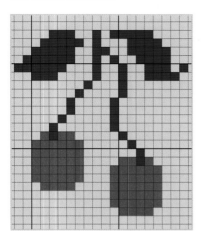

← **Box chart:** There are many books containing needlepoint designs in chart form, with yarn or thread colors specified. A box chart is most often used for designs worked in tent stitch; each box in the chart represents one stitch. The thread colors can be represented either by printed colors or by symbols or, sometimes (in complex designs), by both.

→ **Line chart:** A line chart is most often used for designs consisting of, or including, novelty stitches. The lines of the grid represent the actual canvas threads and the stitches are marked on top of them.

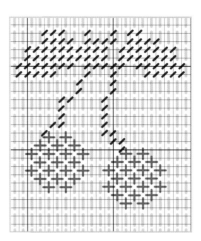

Your own designs

Don't be afraid of creating your own needlepoint designs; it's not as hard as you may think. Once you start looking for ideas, you'll find them all around you—in nature, in paintings and photographs, and in the textures of needlepoint stitches themselves.

NEEDLEPOINT SAMPLERS

Begin by making a sampler of some of your favorite stitches. Work a few of each of these on spare canvas and study their shape and texture. Select a few harmonizing and/or contrasting colors of thread and work stripes of the various stitches in these colors across a narrow piece of canvas. Alternatively, work stripes concentrically around a small block of stitches (cushion stitch, for example). Keep adding stripes until the work is large enough to make the front of a cushion cover.

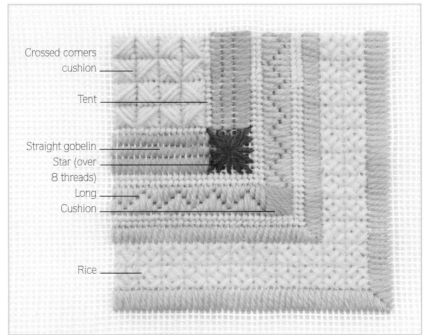

Crossed corners cushion

Tent

Straight gobelin
Star (over 8 threads)
Long
Cushion

Rice

DESIGNING WITH SHAPES

You can create both abstract and pictorial designs with cutout shapes. For an abstract design, cut some squares, rectangles, triangles, or circles from colored paper. Draw the area of the finished needlepoint on a sheet of paper. Move the shapes around on this area, trying different combinations until you find one that pleases you. Remember to pay attention to the spaces between the shapes; these are an important part of any design. Attach the shapes with adhesive putty and leave the design for a few hours, then come back and look at it with fresh eyes.

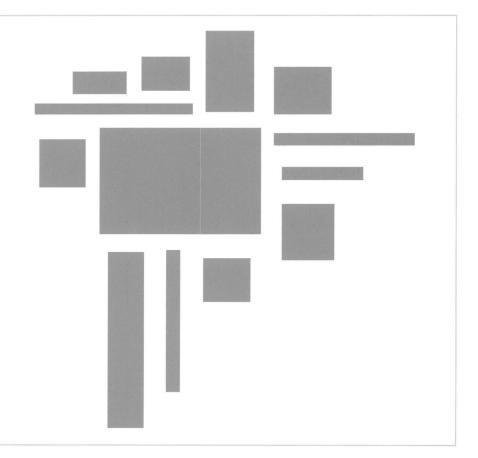

USING CROSS-STITCH MOTIFS

You can find hundreds of appealing cross-stitch motifs in books. Draw one on a piece of graph paper containing the same number of lines as your chosen canvas, or repeat a small one across the area of the grid.

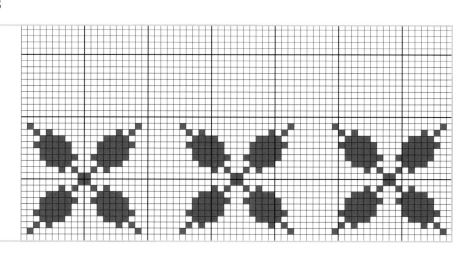

CHARTING FROM AN IMAGE

To create more realistic pictorial designs, either draw or paint the design freehand or follow these instructions to make a chart from an existing image.

1 Isolate an image from a larger source by moving strips of paper over the image until you find the best detail for your project. Enlarge the detail on a photocopier to the desired size.

2 To make a chart, place gridded tracing paper over the image and then fill in the squares on the tracing paper, using colored pencils. Or, if you are using textured stitches, indicate these with lines.

TIPS

• **To make an** entirely original needlepoint, start with your own drawing or painting. If you lack confidence, practice! Carry a sketchbook around with you and sketch interesting shapes and textures. Make a note of colors and develop your sketches in color when you get home. Use strips of paper (see above) to find interesting details that can be enlarged.

• **As you can** see from the stitches illustrated on pages 160–191, needlepoint stitches have their own distinctive character—some smooth and shiny, some bumpy, some with a strong vertical, horizontal, or diagonal direction. You can exploit this in your design. For example, you might use encroaching gobelin (see page 165) in shades of blue to depict sky; stem stitch (see page 171) for a field of corn; or straight cross (see page 179) for a pebbly beach.

Transferring techniques

If you are working from a chart (see page 145), the process of counting the lines/blocks of the chart and the canvas threads will transfer the design as you stitch. Otherwise, you will need to trace or paint the design onto the canvas.

TRACING OUTLINES

1 Begin by going over the outlines of your design with a black felt-tip marker. Choose a marker that is thick enough to be visible through your chosen canvas. Using the same marker, draw an outline enclosing the area to be stitched.

3 Tape or weight the design onto a flat, hard surface, and position the canvas on top; tape it in place. Trace the design outlines onto the canvas using a permanent fabric marker.

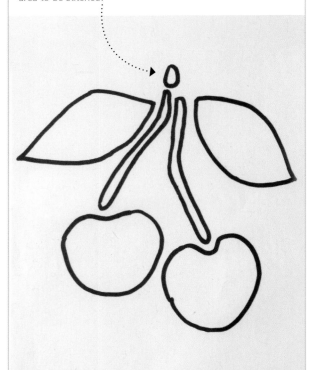

2 Prepare the canvas: cut it to size, adding at least 4in (10cm) to the dimensions of the area to be stitched. Using a permanent fabric marker, draw the outline of this area in the center of the canvas, leaving a 2in (5cm) border all around. Cover the edges with masking tape.

4 If your design is colored you may wish to color in the outlines on the canvas, too. Use permanent acrylic paints for this. Avoid clogging the mesh with paint and leave the canvas to dry thoroughly.

Choosing the right canvas

In choosing canvas for a project you need to consider its type, its gauge, and its color. For most projects an ordinary single-thread canvas will be suitable, but in some cases an interlock or double canvas will be preferable or even required. If you wish to use a certain kind of thread, this may limit the choice of gauge. The predominant color tones of the work may influence the color of canvas you choose.

FOR USING HALF-CROSS STITCH

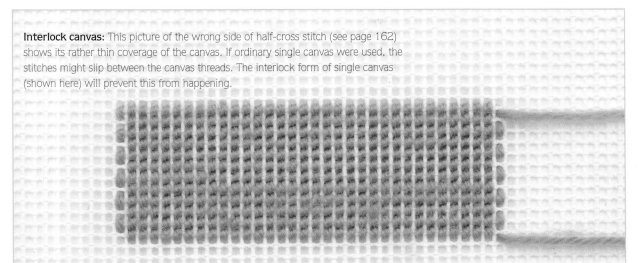

Interlock canvas: This picture of the wrong side of half-cross stitch (see page 162) shows its rather thin coverage of the canvas. If ordinary single canvas were used, the stitches might slip between the canvas threads. The interlock form of single canvas (shown here) will prevent this from happening.

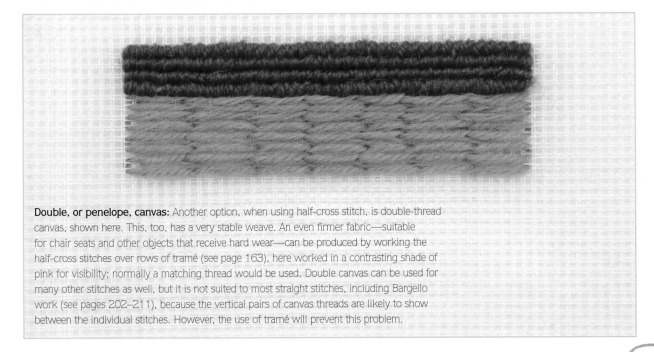

Double, or penelope, canvas: Another option, when using half-cross stitch, is double-thread canvas, shown here. This, too, has a very stable weave. An even firmer fabric—suitable for chair seats and other objects that receive hard wear—can be produced by working the half-cross stitches over rows of tramé (see page 163), here worked in a contrasting shade of pink for visibility; normally a matching thread would be used. Double canvas can be used for many other stitches as well, but it is not suited to most straight stitches, including Bargello work (see pages 202–211), because the vertical pairs of canvas threads are likely to show between the individual stitches. However, the use of tramé will prevent this problem.

CHOOSING THE RIGHT GAUGE FOR THE CHOSEN THREAD

If you wish to use a single strand of thread for the stitching, this will limit your choice of gauge. The thread should fill the hole comfortably—neither too tightly, which would produce a lumpy, distorted surface, nor loosely, which would produce a thin effect. A few successful combinations are shown here.

Tapestry yarn is suitable for 10-, 12-, or 14-count canvas (if tent stitch is used).

Pearl cotton (No. 5) works well on 18-count canvas.

A single strand of Persian yarn will also cover the mesh of an 18-count canvas.

CHOOSING THE RIGHT GAUGE FOR THE AMOUNT OF DETAIL

10-count canvas

Another consideration

is the amount of detail you wish to include. The finer the canvas, the more detail you can include and the more easily you can represent curved lines.

18-count canvas

These two monograms,

for example, are based on the same printed source and were first charted onto graph paper having 10 and 18 squares to 1 in (2.5cm). The finer grid and canvas mesh allows a more faithful representation of the curves. However, the more angular "S" has a certain appeal and might be the sort of look you are aiming for. A lot depends on the nature of the design material.

Matching thread and canvas

For most projects, you'll want to choose a thread that covers the canvas well. This depends partly on the stitches you plan to use: a dense stitch such as tent (see pages 161–162) will cover better than a less-dense one, such as long stitch (see page 177), using the same thread and canvas. Before beginning a project, make some samples to ensure that your chosen materials and stitches are compatible.

This chart provides a guide to choosing suitable yarns for working tent stitch (either continental or basketweave) on various gauges of canvas. (English crewel yarn is assumed; for French crewel, more strands may be required.)

GAUGE OF CANVAS	TYPE AND NUMBER OF STRANDS
10-count	1 strand of tapestry yarn 2 strands of Persian yarn 4 strands of crewel yarn
12-count	1 strand of tapestry yarn 2 strands of Persian yarn 3 strands of crewel yarn
14-count	1 strand of tapestry yarn 2 strands of Persian yarn 3 strands of crewel yarn
18-count	1 strand of No. 5 pearl cotton 1 strand of Persian yarn 2 strands of crewel yarn 6 strands of stranded floss

Estimating thread quantities

If your design uses a large area of a single color, buy enough yarn or thread at the outset to avoid changes in dye lots. The following amounts are based on basketweave tent stitch (see page 161) worked on single-thread canvas, using 18in (45cm) lengths and allowing about 3in (8cm) waste per thread. If you are using half-cross stitch (see page 162), divide the amounts by one half.

GAUGE OF CANVAS	TYPE AND NUMBER OF STRANDS
10-count	6yd (5.5m) to 4sq in (25sq cm)
12-count	6½yd (6m) to 4sq in (25sq cm)
14-count	7½yd (7m) to 4sq in (25sq cm)
16-count	8yd (7.5m) to 4sq in (25sq cm)
18-count	10yd (9m) to 4sq in (25sq cm)

CHOOSING THE CANVAS COLOR

Woven canvas is available in tan, yellow, cream, and white. The choice depends partly on personal preference (threads are easiest to count on white but tan is easier on the eyes) and partly on the predominating colors of the yarns. White or cream canvas would be a good choice for a piece worked in pastel colors, whereas tan would be more suitable for darker hues.

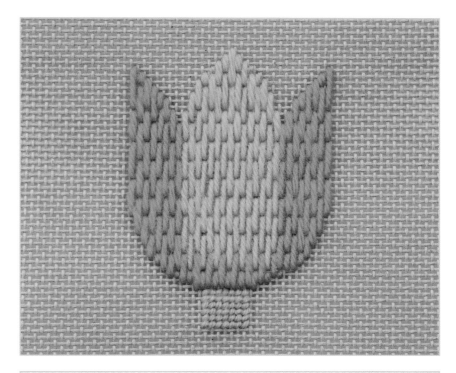

In this example, the same yarn and stitches worked on white canvas are less successful than they are in the tulip worked on tan canvas. The color is more important for straight stitches (here gobelin filling) than for diagonal ones, such as continental or basketweave tent.

Getting started

Before beginning to stitch a commercially printed canvas, all you need to do is bind the edges with masking tape, although you may wish also to mount the canvas on a frame. To follow a chart you need to cut the canvas to size first.

Preparing the canvas

If you are following a chart or creating your own design, a few more preliminary steps are involved. Make a note of the canvas measurements and keep this handy, since you will need it for blocking the finished work (see page 192). If you have drawn or painted your own design on the canvas, you can treat it as you would a commercially printed canvas and simply begin stitching after binding the edges.

MARKING AND CUTTING THE CANVAS

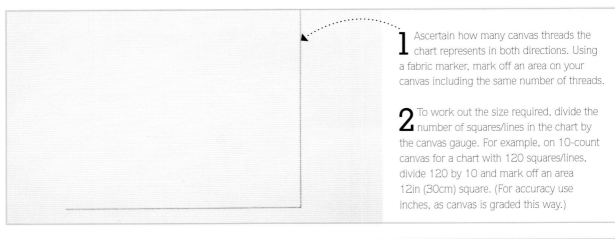

1 Ascertain how many canvas threads the chart represents in both directions. Using a fabric marker, mark off an area on your canvas including the same number of threads.

2 To work out the size required, divide the number of squares/lines in the chart by the canvas gauge. For example, on 10-count canvas for a chart with 120 squares/lines, divide 120 by 10 and mark off an area 12in (30cm) square. (For accuracy use inches, as canvas is graded this way.)

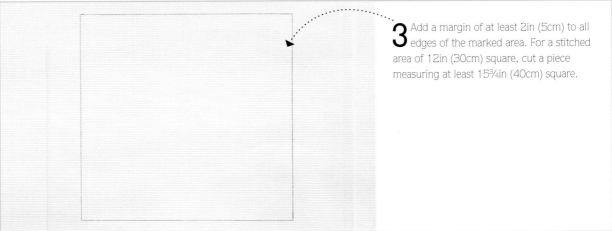

3 Add a margin of at least 2in (5cm) to all edges of the marked area. For a stitched area of 12in (30cm) square, cut a piece measuring at least 15¾in (40cm) square.

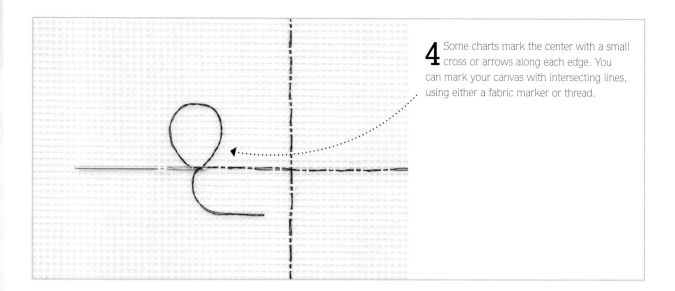

4 Some charts mark the center with a small cross or arrows along each edge. You can mark your canvas with intersecting lines, using either a fabric marker or thread.

BINDING THE EDGES

Whether working on a preprinted or blank canvas, you need to bind the edges using masking tape. Alternatively, bind them with woven tape. The bound edges are cut off when your project is complete.

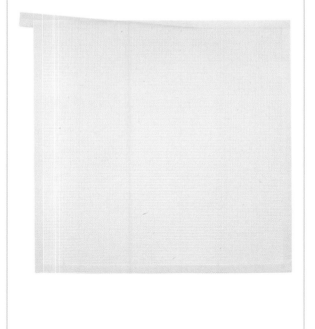

Cut a strip of masking tape slightly longer than one edge. Lay the canvas on a flat surface and gently stick the tape on top, overlapping the edge by about half. Fold the tape to the other side and press in place. Trim the ends. Repeat on all edges.

Mounting canvas on a frame

The use of a frame is optional. A small piece of work, or one using stitches that are unlikely to distort the canvas, can be held in the hand. However, using a frame will help you to maintain a smooth stitching tension.

USING ARTIST'S STRETCHERS

1 Slot the mitered ends together to form a square or rectangle.

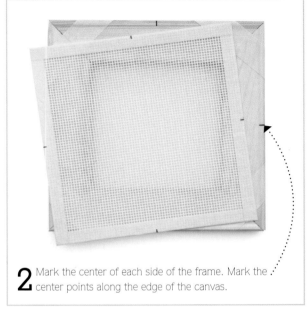

2 Mark the center of each side of the frame. Mark the center points along the edge of the canvas.

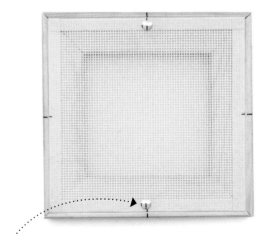

3 Align the center of the top edge of the canvas with the center of the top of the frame. Attach the canvas to the frame at this point with a thumbtack. Repeat at the bottom edge, pulling the canvas taut.

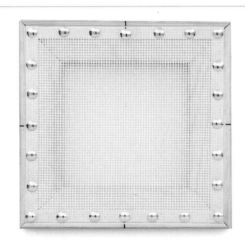

4 Repeat on adjacent sides. Working outward from the center and pulling the canvas taut, insert more thumbtacks along all edges at ¾in (2cm) intervals.

USING A SCROLL FRAME

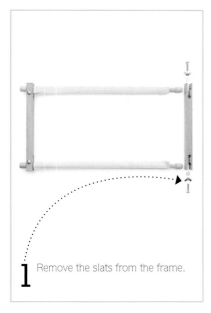

1 Remove the slats from the frame.

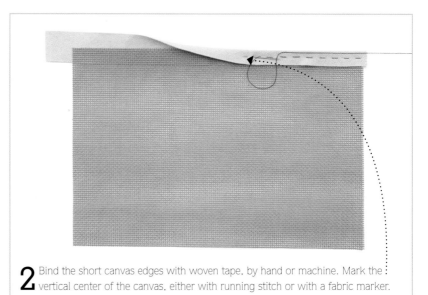

2 Bind the short canvas edges with woven tape, by hand or machine. Mark the vertical center of the canvas, either with running stitch or with a fabric marker.

3 Fold under ¾in (2cm) along the top edge. Using a strong thread, oversew the canvas to the webbing on 1 roller, starting at the matched center points. Work out from the center to the other edge. Repeat for the bottom.

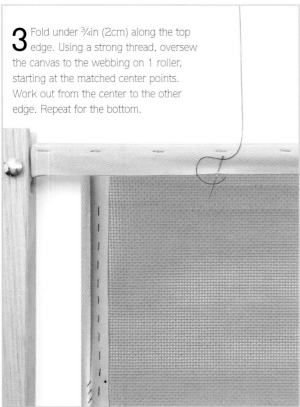

4 Insert the slats into the rollers and fasten to stretch the canvas taut. Cut a long length of string and fasten to 1 top corner of the frame. Working over the slats and through the canvas and binding tape, sew the canvas to the slats. Fasten off. Repeat on the opposite side.

Starting to stitch

You have got your design and your thread and you've prepared your canvas. Now you just need to thread a tapestry needle and start stitching (see tips below). There are several ways of getting thick or multistranded threads through the eye of a needle.

TIPS

• **To sew or stab?** Whether you stitch with a horizontal (sewing) or a vertical (stabbing) movement is a matter of personal preference. With stabbing it is generally easier to avoid pulling the canvas out of shape. If you use a self-supporting frame you can work with one hand above the canvas and one below, and so will handle the work less, which helps to keep it clean.

• **Practice stitching** with a smooth, even tension; avoid pulling the stitches too tightly.

• **Wherever possible,** take the needle down—rather than up—through a hole that already contains a thread; this tends to produce a neater effect.

• **To thread stranded floss,** flatten the strands between your tongue and upper teeth and then between forefinger and thumb. A needle threader may also be helpful.

• **Avoid using too long a thread.** About 18in (45cm) is the maximum recommended for crewel or tapestry yarn; Persian yarn may be cut longer because it is more robust.

• **Most of the stitch** descriptions and illustrations on pages 160–211 assume a right-handed stitcher. You can reverse the direction of stitching (try turning the book upside down) or use the stabbing method, or both.

THREADING THE NEEDLE: PAPER STRIP METHOD

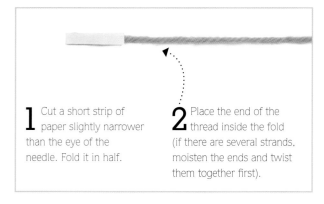

1 Cut a short strip of paper slightly narrower than the eye of the needle. Fold it in half.

2 Place the end of the thread inside the fold (if there are several strands, moisten the ends and twist them together first).

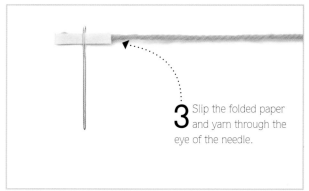

3 Slip the folded paper and yarn through the eye of the needle.

THREADING THE NEEDLE: LOOP METHOD

1 This method, too, can be used for 1 or more strands. Loop the strands around the needle and pinch the loops tightly together.

2 Slip the needle out of the loops, then push the eye down over them. Once the loops emerge, pull them through the eye of the needle.

Starting and ending a thread

In order to avoid unsightly bumps or fluffy strands of thread on your finished piece of needlepoint, you need to start and end the thread neatly, securing it on the back of the canvas to prevent your work from unraveling.

STARTING A THREAD ON EMPTY CANVAS

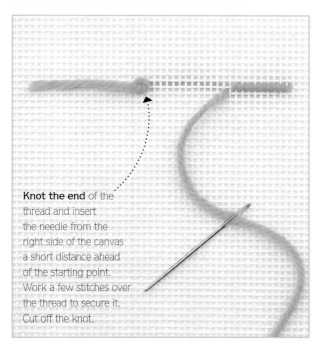

Knot the end of the thread and insert the needle from the right side of the canvas a short distance ahead of the starting point. Work a few stitches over the thread to secure it. Cut off the knot.

ENDING A THREAD

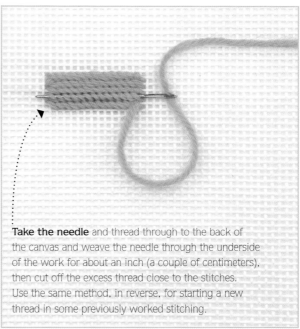

Take the needle and thread through to the back of the canvas and weave the needle through the underside of the work for about an inch (a couple of centimeters), then cut off the excess thread close to the stitches. Use the same method, in reverse, for starting a new thread in some previously worked stitching.

STARTING A THREAD ON PLASTIC CANVAS

On plastic canvas, work a couple of backstitches through the mesh 1½–2in (4–5cm) from the starting point, leaving a short tail at the front. Work your chosen stitch almost up to the backstitches. Undo these fastening stitches, pull the tail to the wrong side, and cut it off. For extra security, leave a longer tail, hold it in place at the back, and then thread it back through the stitches of the next row.

Needlepoint stitches

A design can be worked using a single stitch or several different stitches. Pictorial designs are often worked entirely in tent stitch (also called *petit point*), whereas the larger-scale textured stitches generally lend themselves better to abstract designs. Experiment with these stitches to discover their character.

Diagonal stitches

All of these stitches involve crossing at least one thread intersection, or mesh, producing a diagonal effect. Work with a relaxed tension or on a frame to avoid distorting the canvas. Unless otherwise stated, either single or double canvas can be used.

CONTINENTAL TENT STITCH

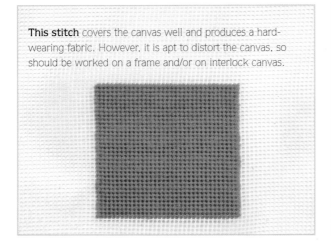

This stitch covers the canvas well and produces a hard-wearing fabric. However, it is apt to distort the canvas, so should be worked on a frame and/or on interlock canvas.

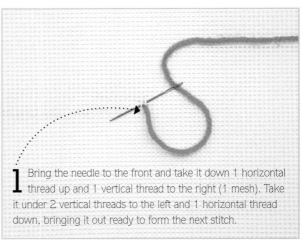

1 Bring the needle to the front and take it down 1 horizontal thread up and 1 vertical thread to the right (1 mesh). Take it under 2 vertical threads to the left and 1 horizontal thread down, bringing it out ready to form the next stitch.

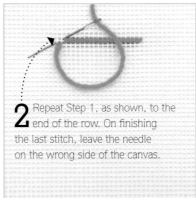

2 Repeat Step 1, as shown, to the end of the row. On finishing the last stitch, leave the needle on the wrong side of the canvas.

3 For the next row, work back alongside the first row, bringing the needle up into the holes occupied by the stitches of the first row. On alternate rows work down into holes used in the previous row.

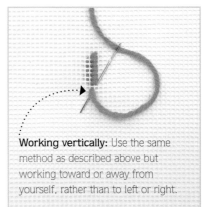

Working vertically: Use the same method as described above but working toward or away from yourself, rather than to left or right.

BASKETWEAVE STITCH

Also called diagonal tent because of the woven effect produced on the wrong side, this stitch is recommended for larger areas of a single color. For practice, begin at the top right-hand corner as shown here.

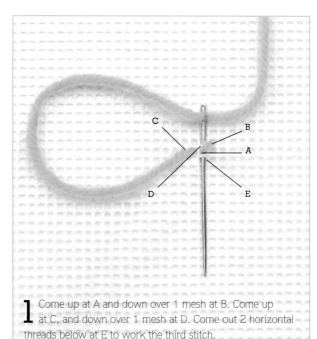

1 Come up at A and down over 1 mesh at B. Come up at C, and down over 1 mesh at D. Come out 2 horizontal threads below at E to work the third stitch.

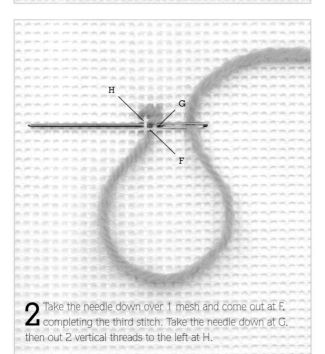

2 Take the needle down over 1 mesh and come out at F, completing the third stitch. Take the needle down at G, then out 2 vertical threads to the left at H.

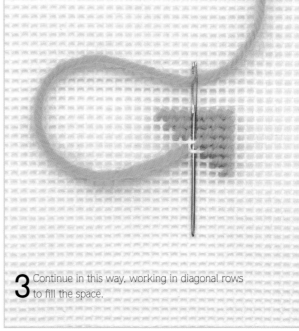

3 Continue in this way, working in diagonal rows to fill the space.

DIAGONAL LINES OF TENT STITCH

Lines of tent stitch from upper right to lower left,
or upper left to lower right, are essentially backstitch, taking
the needle over 1 mesh and under 2 each time. If using the
sewing method of stitching (see page 159), turn the work
90 degrees for one or other of these directions, depending
on whether you are right- or left-handed.

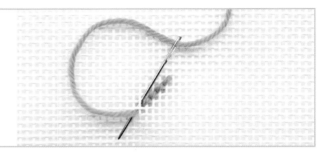

HALF-CROSS STITCH

This stitch looks almost the same on the right side as
continental or basketweave stitch, but on the wrong
side the threads do not completely cover the canvas, and
so the resulting fabric is not so strong. Use interlock,
double, or plastic canvas for this stitch.

Wrong side

1 Bring the needle to front and take
it down over 1 mesh up and to
the right (A). Take it under 1 thread
(or double thread) immediately
below, ready to begin next stitch.

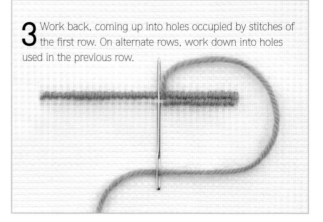

A

2 Repeat Step 1
across the row as
shown. At the end of
row, leave needle on
wrong side of canvas.

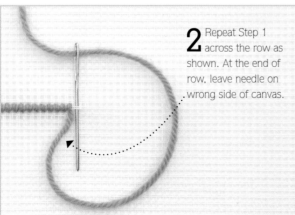

3 Work back, coming up into holes occupied by stitches of
the first row. On alternate rows, work down into holes
used in the previous row.

TRAMÉ

Tramé (or tramming) is a technique of laying long horizontal stitches to provide a foundation for other stitches, such as half-cross stitch on double canvas, or gobelin stitch on single canvas.

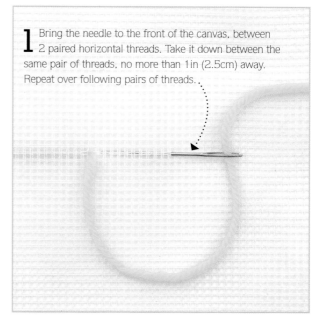

1 Bring the needle to the front of the canvas, between 2 paired horizontal threads. Take it down between the same pair of threads, no more than 1in (2.5cm) away. Repeat over following pairs of threads.

2 If additional width is needed, bring the needle up to the left of where the first tramé stitch ended, under 1 vertical canvas thread, splitting the yarn. Continue across required width.

3 Work the chosen stitches over the tramé; here, half-cross stitch is shown, using a contrasting color for clarity.

BEADED TENT STITCH

For additional texture you can add beads to tent stitch or half-cross stitch. Choose beads with holes large enough for your thread. For solid bead work, choose beads the same size as the stitches.

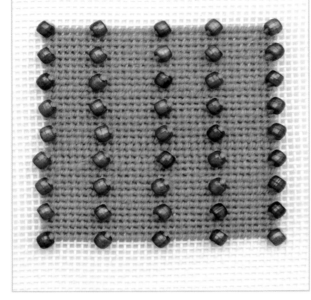

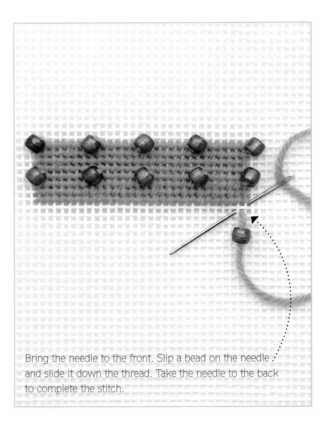

Bring the needle to the front. Slip a bead on the needle and slide it down the thread. Take the needle to the back to complete the stitch.

SLANTED GOBELIN STITCH

This easy stitch is ideal for backgrounds. The horizontal, ridged effect can be enhanced with tramé.

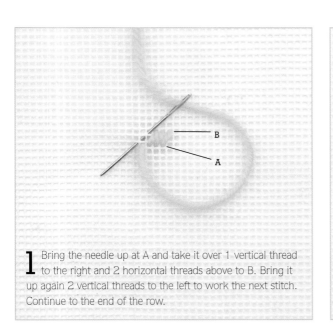

1 Bring the needle up at A and take it over 1 vertical thread to the right and 2 horizontal threads above to B. Bring it up again 2 vertical threads to the left to work the next stitch. Continue to the end of the row.

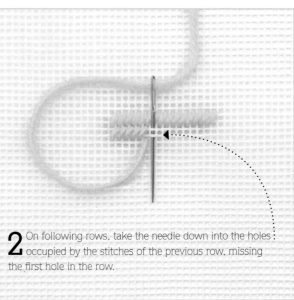

2 On following rows, take the needle down into the holes occupied by the stitches of the previous row, missing the first hole in the row.

ENCROACHING GOBELIN STITCH

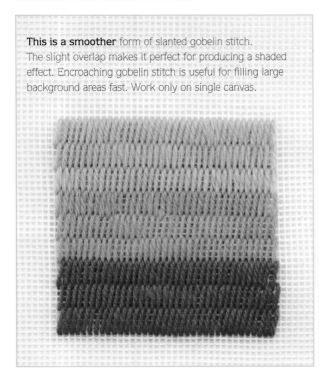

This is a smoother form of slanted gobelin stitch. The slight overlap makes it perfect for producing a shaded effect. Encroaching gobelin stitch is useful for filling large background areas fast. Work only on single canvas.

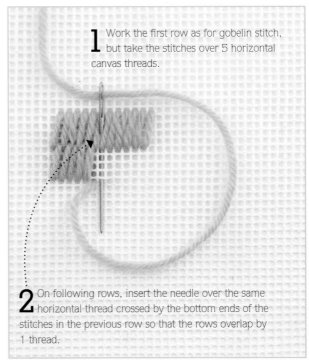

1 Work the first row as for gobelin stitch, but take the stitches over 5 horizontal canvas threads.

2 On following rows, insert the needle over the same horizontal thread crossed by the bottom ends of the stitches in the previous row so that the rows overlap by 1 thread.

CUSHION STITCH

Also called squares pattern or flat stitch, this is made of graduated diagonal stitches that form squares. The stitches of adjacent squares slant in opposite directions, giving the work a strong textural effect.

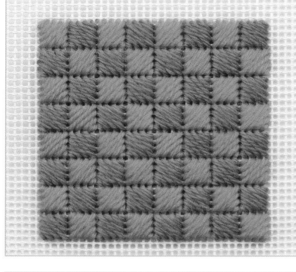

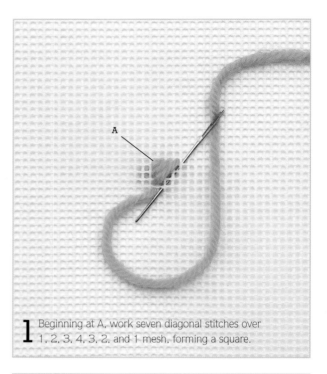

1 Beginning at A, work seven diagonal stitches over 1, 2, 3, 4, 3, 2, and 1 mesh, forming a square.

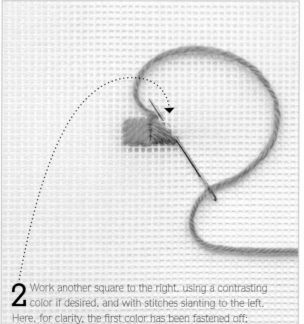

2 Work another square to the right, using a contrasting color if desired, and with stitches slanting to the left. Here, for clarity, the first color has been fastened off; normally you would use 2 needles and colors alternately.

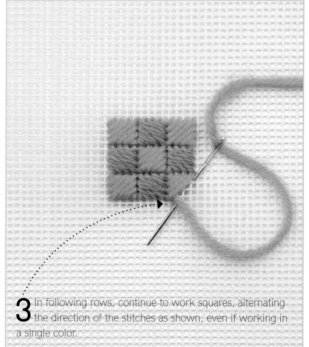

3 In following rows, continue to work squares, alternating the direction of the stitches as shown, even if working in a single color.

CHECKER STITCH

Used for covering large areas, this stitch can be worked in two (or more) colors to enhance the checkerboard effect, or in one color to emphasize the textural contrast.

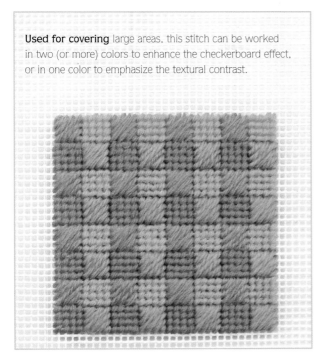

1 Starting at A, work 7 graduated diagonal stitches over 1, 2, 3, 4, 3, 2, and 1 mesh, forming a square.

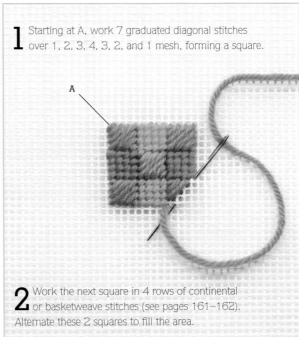

2 Work the next square in 4 rows of continental or basketweave stitches (see pages 161–162). Alternate these 2 squares to fill the area.

SCOTTISH STITCH

This stitch forms a lattice effect. Although it can be worked in a single color, the effect is more pronounced if contrasting colors or different textures of thread are used.

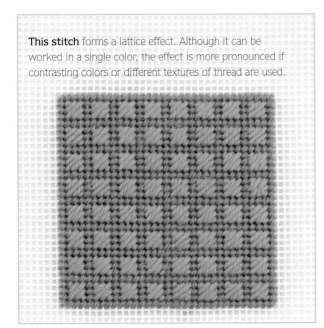

1 Work a block of 5 diagonal stitches over 3 horizontal and 3 vertical threads. Work more blocks, slanting the stitches in the same direction, leaving 1 canvas thread free between the blocks.

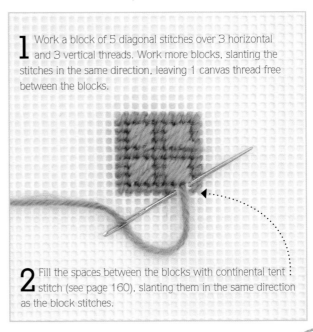

2 Fill the spaces between the blocks with continental tent stitch (see page 160), slanting them in the same direction as the block stitches.

MOSAIC STITCH

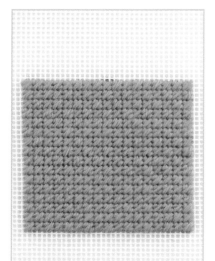

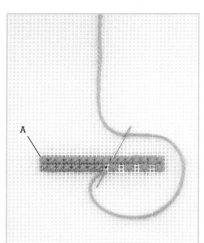

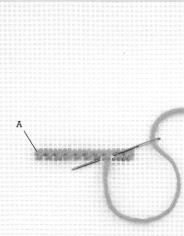

Worked in two colors, mosaic stitch forms a checkerboard pattern. It can also be worked in a single color, producing a subtle texture.

Checkerboard: Starting at A in first color, work block of 3 stitches over 2 vertical and 2 horizontal threads. Leave 2 vertical threads. Work next block. Fill in with second color.

Single color: Work in rows, starting at A. Work all top short stitches and longer stitches across a row. Fill in the bottom short stitches on the next row.

DIAGONAL STITCH

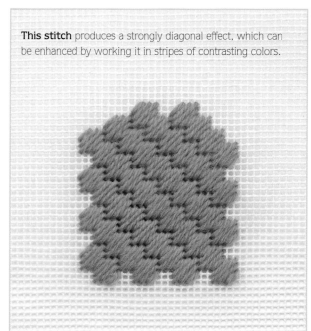

This stitch produces a strongly diagonal effect, which can be enhanced by working it in stripes of contrasting colors.

1 Work each row from top left to bottom right. Come up at A, take the needle over 2, 3, 4, and 3 mesh. Repeat sequence.

2 On subsequent rows, fit the stitches together as shown, with 4-mesh stitches next to 2-mesh stitches and vice versa.

MOORISH STITCH

This stitch is a combination of interlocked squares, worked on the diagonal, and tent stitches. Worked in contrasting colors, the effect is a zigzag striped pattern.

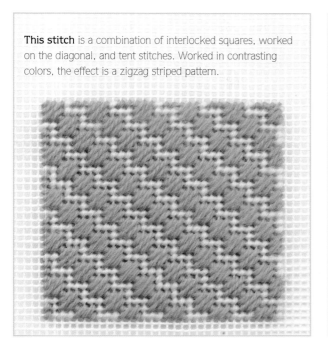

1 Starting at A, work 4 diagonal stitches over 1, 2, 3, and 2 mesh. Repeat the sequence to the end.

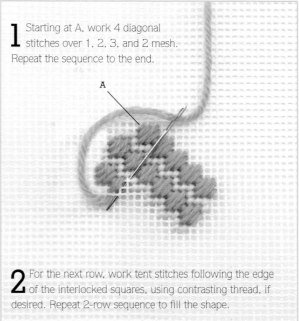

2 For the next row, work tent stitches following the edge of the interlocked squares, using contrasting thread, if desired. Repeat 2-row sequence to fill the shape.

BYZANTINE STITCH

Useful for filling large areas, Byzantine stitch forms a bold stepped pattern with a satiny texture.

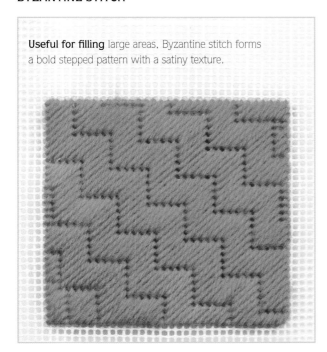

1 Work from lower right to upper left, starting at A. Take needle over 4 vertical and 4 horizontal threads. Work 5 more identical stitches above. Change direction, working 5 stitches horizontally to the left, then 5 vertically, and so on as required.

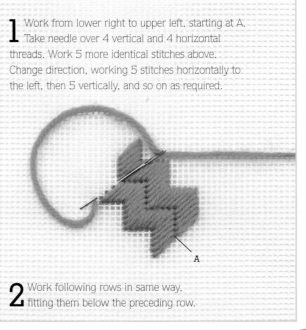

2 Work following rows in same way, fitting them below the preceding row.

JACQUARD STITCH

The step pattern of Jacquard stitch is accentuated by using contrasting colors or combining matte and shiny threads.

1 Work from lower right to upper left. Wider rows are worked over 2 horizontal and 2 vertical threads. Each step consists of 5 stitches.

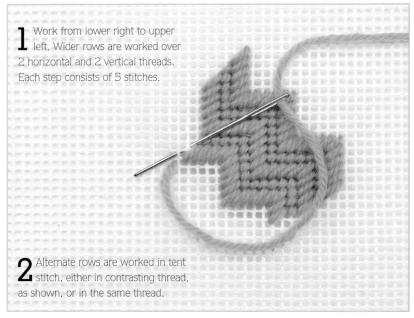

2 Alternate rows are worked in tent stitch, either in contrasting thread, as shown, or in the same thread.

MILANESE STITCH

This stitch is constructed of interlocking triangles worked in backstitch. It is excellent for backgrounds.

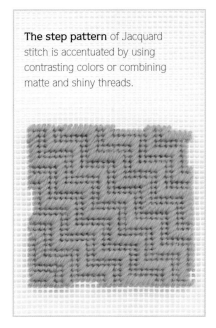

1 Start at A. Work diagonal stitches over 1, 2, 3, and 4 mesh to form a triangle.

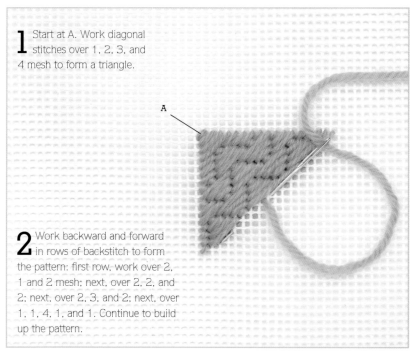

2 Work backward and forward in rows of backstitch to form the pattern: first row, work over 2, 1 and 2 mesh; next, over 2, 2, and 2; next, over 2, 3, and 2; next, over 1, 1, 4, 1, and 1. Continue to build up the pattern.

ORIENTAL STITCH

This scaled-up version of Milanese stitch (see opposite) is useful for filling backgrounds. It can be worked in one color, but its structure is easier to grasp if practiced in two colors.

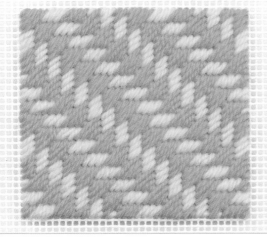

1 Work rows of triangles over 1, 2, 3, and 4 mesh, with rows of triangles pointing up and down alternately and bases touching.

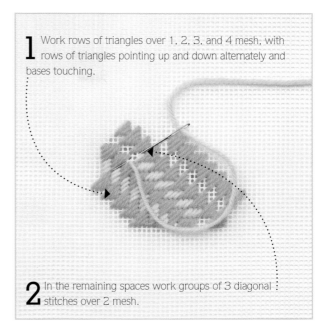

2 In the remaining spaces work groups of 3 diagonal stitches over 2 mesh.

STEM STITCH

This attractive stitch is suggestive of grass or wheat. The diagonal stitches can be used on their own, but working lines of backstitch between them in a contrasting color accentuates the vertical quality.

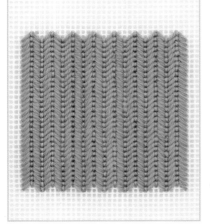

1 Beginning at A, work a diagonal stitch over 2 mesh. Continue to the top, then work down alongside these stitches, slanting the next row in the opposite direction. Work rows across the canvas.

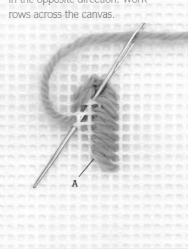

2 Using a contrasting thread, if desired, work backstitches between the rows of diagonal stitches.

CROSSED CORNERS CUSHION STITCH

This pretty variation of cushion stitch (see page 166). is produced by covering half of a square with diagonal stitches worked at a right angle to the first ones. Many different effects can be created by varying the positions of the top stitches.

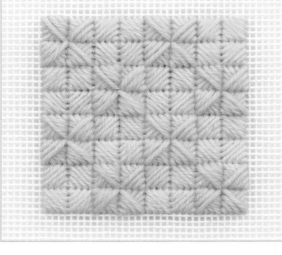

1 Work a square of cushion stitch over 4 threads. After working the last corner stitch, bring the needle up in the hole just above the first corner stitch.

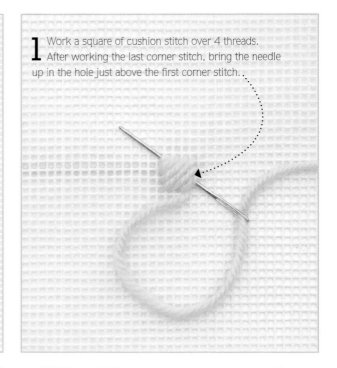

2 Work 4 diagonal stitches to cover ½ of the block. Bring the needle up 5 vertical threads to the left at A. Work another cushion stitch in the same direction as the previously worked crossing stitches.

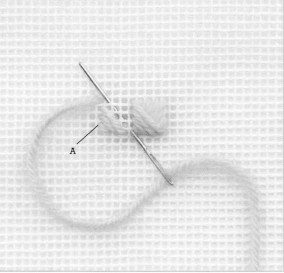

A

3 Cross the inner corner of this square as for the previous one. Continuing in a counterclockwise direction, work 2 more squares with crossed corners.

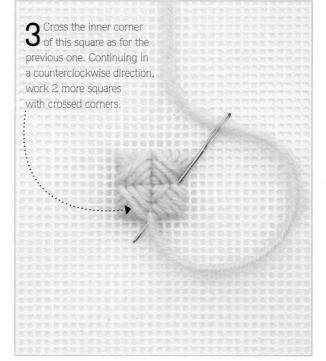

Straight stitches

All of the stitches in this section are formed by working in a vertical or horizontal direction. Most of them are easy to work; in fact, many needlepoint kits are worked in a modified form of long stitch (see page 177) that covers the canvas very quickly. However, you should avoid using very long stitches for an object that will receive wear, since they are likely to snag. All the stitches in this section are best worked on single canvas.

STRAIGHT GOBELIN STITCH

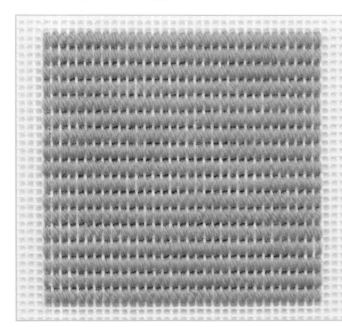

This **simple stitch** is useful for backgrounds. If worked over 2 horizontal threads, it produces a ridged appearance. This effect can be enhanced by working it over tramé (see page 163). For a flatter, glossier effect, work over 3 or 4 threads.

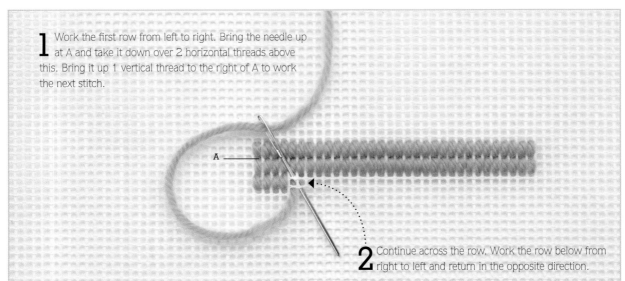

1 Work the first row from left to right. Bring the needle up at A and take it down over 2 horizontal threads above this. Bring it up 1 vertical thread to the right of A to work the next stitch.

A

2 Continue across the row. Work the row below from right to left and return in the opposite direction.

INTERLOCKING STRAIGHT GOBELIN

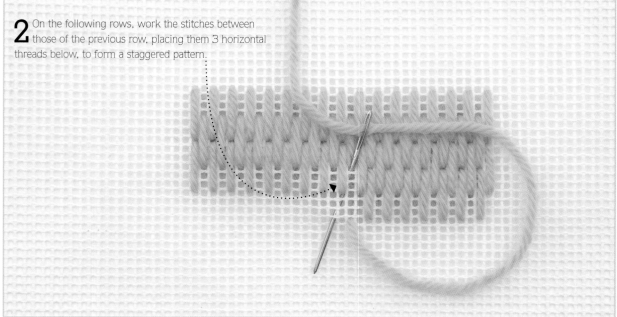

This easy stitch lends itself well to shading. Normally worked over 6 horizontal threads, the same basic method can be used over 4 threads to make a sturdier fabric.

1 Starting at top left (A), or top right, work a row of vertical stitches over 6 horizontal threads, leaving 2 vertical threads between them.

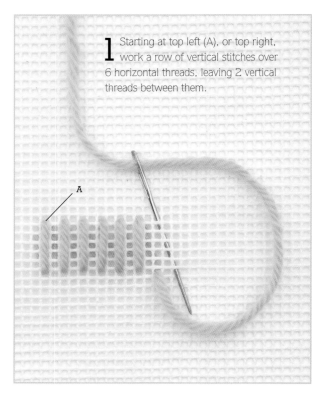

2 On the following rows, work the stitches between those of the previous row, placing them 3 horizontal threads below, to form a staggered pattern.

RANDOM STRAIGHT STITCH

This stitch is especially good for producing shaded effects and suggesting the sky or fields.

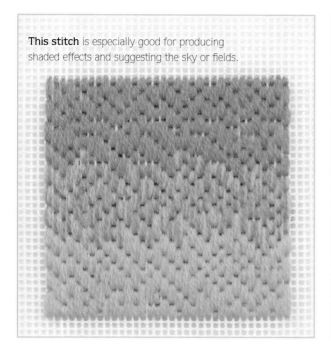

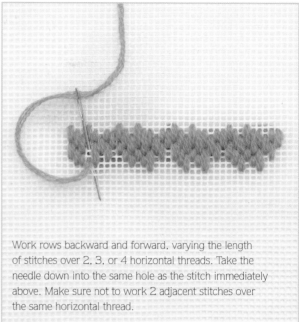

Work rows backward and forward, varying the length of stitches over 2, 3, or 4 horizontal threads. Take the needle down into the same hole as the stitch immediately above. Make sure not to work 2 adjacent stitches over the same horizontal thread.

PARISIAN STITCH

This is good for filling backgrounds and can be used for shaded effects.

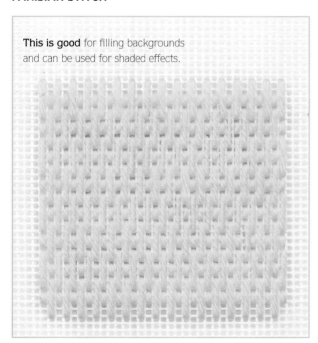

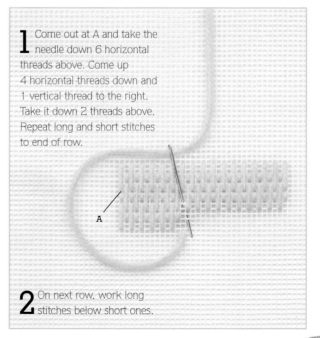

1 Come out at A and take the needle down 6 horizontal threads above. Come up 4 horizontal threads down and 1 vertical thread to the right. Take it down 2 threads above. Repeat long and short stitches to end of row.

A

2 On next row, work long stitches below short ones.

TWILL STITCH

Quick and easy to work, this is a good choice for a smooth background. It has a strongly diagonal feel, resembling the weave of twill fabric.

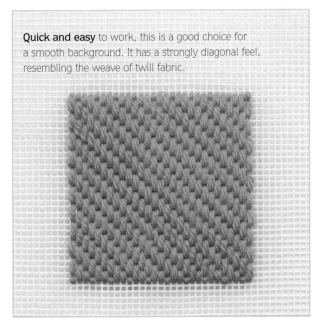

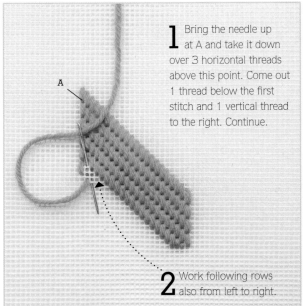

1 Bring the needle up at A and take it down over 3 horizontal threads above this point. Come out 1 thread below the first stitch and 1 vertical thread to the right. Continue.

2 Work following rows also from left to right.

DOUBLE TWILL STITCH

Here, the diagonal feel is accentuated by lines of short stitches alternating with longer ones. This effect can be enhanced by working the short stitches in a different color.

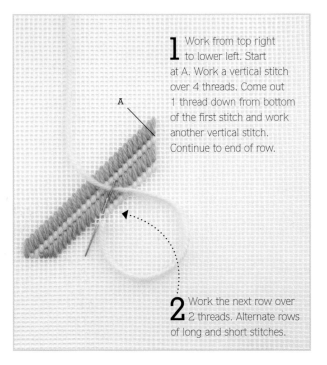

1 Work from top right to lower left. Start at A. Work a vertical stitch over 4 threads. Come out 1 thread down from bottom of the first stitch and work another vertical stitch. Continue to end of row.

2 Work the next row over 2 threads. Alternate rows of long and short stitches.

LONG STITCH

This stitch produces a pattern of interlocking triangles. It is especially attractive worked in a lustrous thread, such as stranded floss.

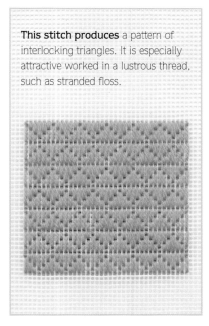

1 Start at top left (A) with a vertical stitch over 1 horizontal thread. Work the following stitches over 2, 3, 4, 3, and 2 threads. Repeat sequence across row.

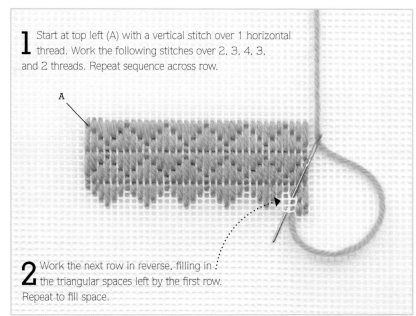

2 Work the next row in reverse, filling in the triangular spaces left by the first row. Repeat to fill space.

PAVILION DIAMOND STITCH

This simple stitch produces a smooth-textured lattice pattern that is good for large areas.

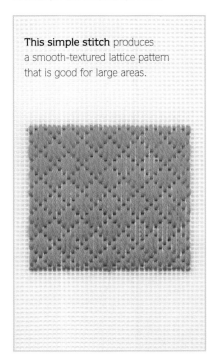

1 Work from right to left from A, working blocks of vertical stitches over 2, 4, 6, 4, and 2 horizontal threads and leaving 2 vertical threads between each block.

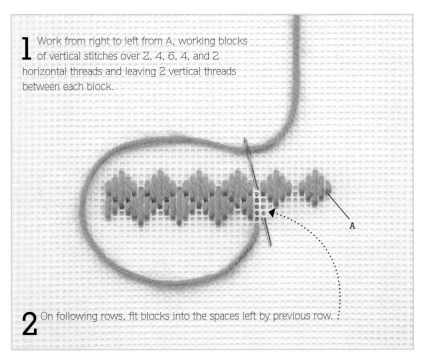

2 On following rows, fit blocks into the spaces left by previous row.

HUNGARIAN STITCH

This stitch may be worked all in one color or, as shown, in two colors for a mosaic effect.

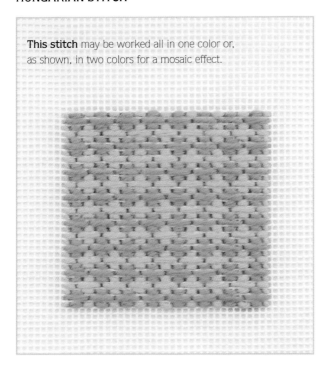

1 Start at A. Work 3 vertical stitches over 2, 4, and 2 horizontal threads. Leave 2 vertical canvas threads and work an identical group of stitches to the right. Repeat to end of row.

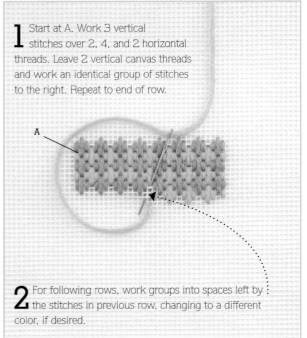

2 For following rows, work groups into spaces left by the stitches in previous row, changing to a different color, if desired.

WEAVING STITCH

This stitch creates the illusion of a woven fabric. It consists of blocks of straight stitches worked in alternating directions.

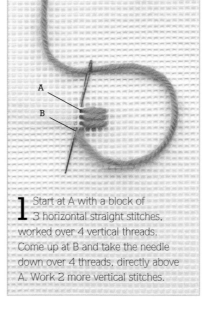

1 Start at A with a block of 3 horizontal straight stitches, worked over 4 vertical threads. Come up at B and take the needle down over 4 threads, directly above A. Work 2 more vertical stitches.

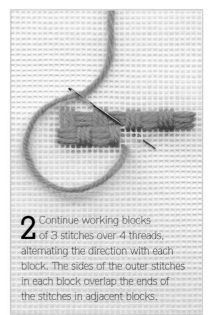

2 Continue working blocks of 3 stitches over 4 threads, alternating the direction with each block. The sides of the outer stitches in each block overlap the ends of the stitches in adjacent blocks.

Crossed stitches

Stitches formed by crossing one thread over another are among the most widely used in needlepoint and create many interesting textures. Some, however, may leave areas of canvas exposed; choose a relatively thick thread to avoid this. Unless otherwise stated, work on either single or double canvas.

CROSS STITCH

Cross stitch is one of the most widely used needlepoint stitches and creates a hard-wearing fabric. You can complete each stitch individually or work it in two stages, as shown.

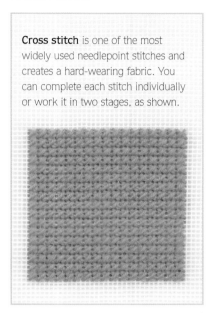

Cross stitch on single canvas: Come up at A. Work a stitch over 2 mesh to upper left. Come out 2 horizontal threads below. Work from right to left. Work back in the opposite direction, crossing first stitches with stitches slanting from lower left to upper right.

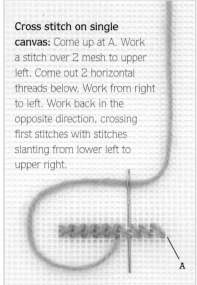

Cross stitch on double canvas: Work as for single canvas, but each stitch is worked over 1 (double) mesh instead of 2. A relatively fine thread should be used; here, Persian yarn is used on 7-count double canvas.

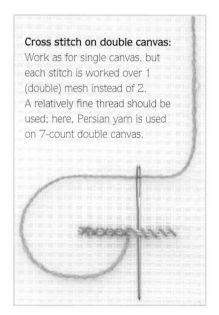

STRAIGHT CROSS STITCH

Despite its small size, this stitch is both useful and attractive, with a nubbly quality that makes it ideal for depicting rough textures.

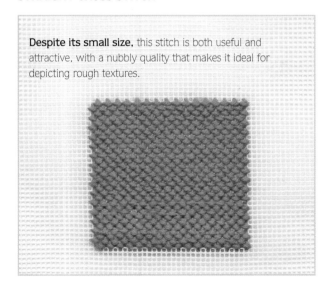

1 Start at A. Work 1 straight stitch over 2 horizontal threads. Cross this with a backstitch over 2 vertical threads. Repeat to end of row.

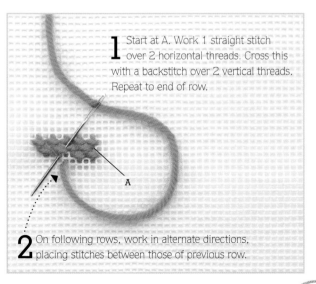

2 On following rows, work in alternate directions, placing stitches between those of previous row.

DIAGONAL CROSS STITCH

This is a series of straight cross stitches separated by diagonal stitches. Work on single canvas.

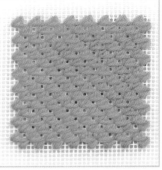

1 Work from lower right to upper left. Come out at A. Take the needle down over 4 horizontal threads above. Bring it up again at A and down over 2 mesh above and to the right. Come out 4 threads to the left at B.

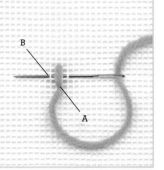

2 Work a horizontal straight stitch, coming up at B to complete first cross and first diagonal stitch. Work a vertical straight stitch over 4 threads, bringing needle out again at B.

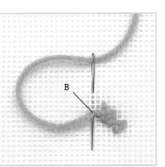

3 Continue working straight cross and diagonal stitches to complete the row. Work following rows under previous ones. Take care that all horizontal stitches lie on top of vertical ones.

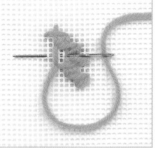

OBLONG CROSS STITCH

This simple variant of basic cross stitch has a ridged appearance and is useful for working borders. Work on single canvas.

1 Work in 2 stages. Starting at A, work a row of diagonal stitches over 4 horizontal and 2 vertical threads.

2 Work back over these stitches in the opposite direction.

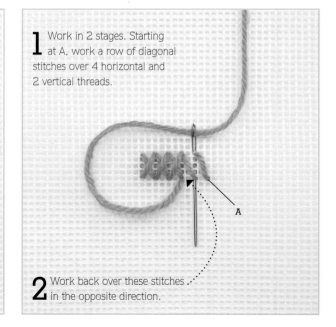

LONG-ARMED CROSS STITCH

This stitch produces an attractive braided effect. Use just a few rows for a border, or more for a background. Work on single canvas.

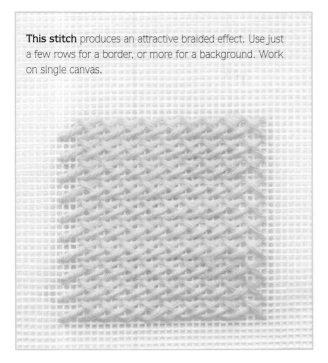

1 Work all rows from left to right. Come up at A and take needle down 6 vertical threads to the right and 3 horizontal threads above. Come up 3 threads below.

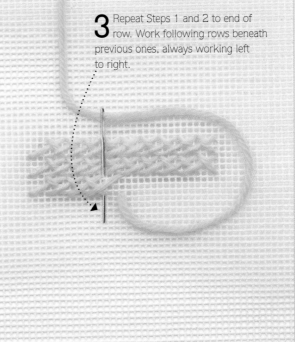

2 Take needle down 3 vertical threads to the left and 3 horizontal threads above. Come up 3 threads below. This completes the first stitch.

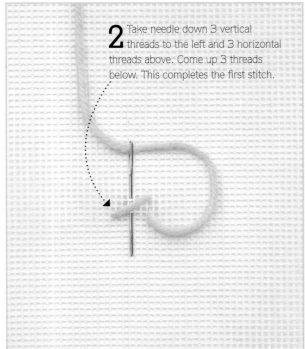

3 Repeat Steps 1 and 2 to end of row. Work following rows beneath previous ones, always working left to right.

ALTERNATING CROSS STITCH

Also known as double stitch, this is good for quickly filling in a background. Work only on single canvas.

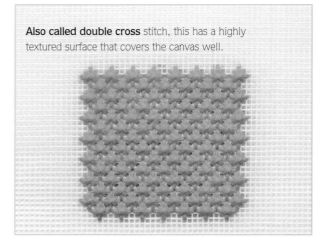

1 Start at A. Work a stitch up over 6 horizontal threads and 2 vertical ones to the left. Come out 6 threads below and take the needle down 6 threads above A.

2 Come out 4 threads below and 2 vertical threads to the left.

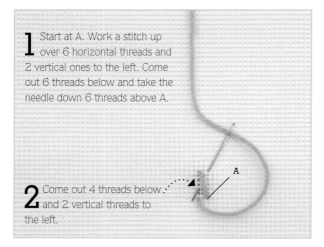

3 Work an ordinary cross stitch (see page 179) over 2 horizontal and 2 vertical threads. Make sure that the top stitch slants to the left. Alternate stitches to end of row.

4 On following rows, place oblong crosses below square ones and vice versa.

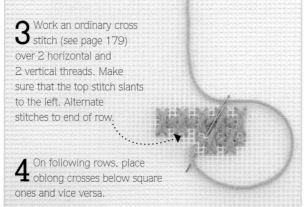

DOUBLE STRAIGHT CROSS STITCH

Also called double cross stitch, this has a highly textured surface that covers the canvas well.

1 Start at A. Work a straight cross stitch over 4 vertical and 4 horizontal canvas threads. Come up 1 mesh below and to the right of center and work an ordinary cross stitch (see page 179) over 4 canvas threads.

2 Work stitches from left to right, with their horizontal arms meeting as shown. On the following row, work from right to left, fitting stitches in between those of previous row.

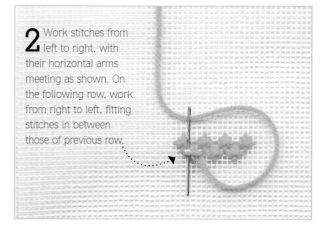

Needlepoint designs

SMYRNA STITCH

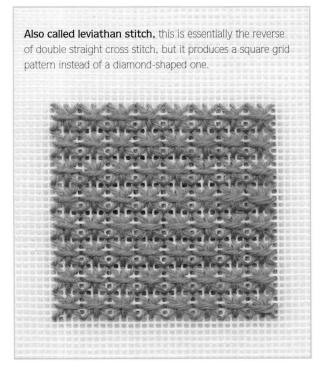

Also called leviathan stitch, this is essentially the reverse of double straight cross stitch, but it produces a square grid pattern instead of a diamond-shaped one.

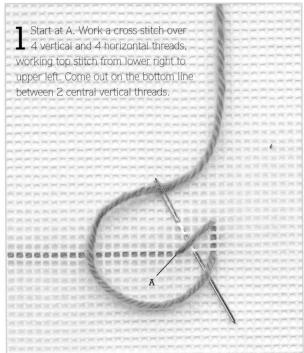

1 Start at A. Work a cross stitch over 4 vertical and 4 horizontal threads, working top stitch from lower right to upper left. Come out on the bottom line between 2 central vertical threads.

A

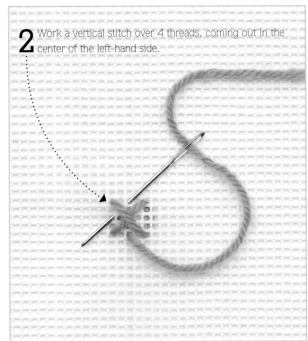

2 Work a vertical stitch over 4 threads, coming out in the center of the left-hand side.

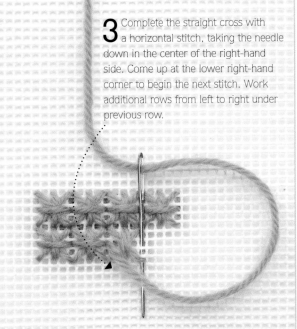

3 Complete the straight cross with a horizontal stitch, taking the needle down in the center of the right-hand side. Come up at the lower right-hand corner to begin the next stitch. Work additional rows from left to right under previous row.

FISHBONE STITCH

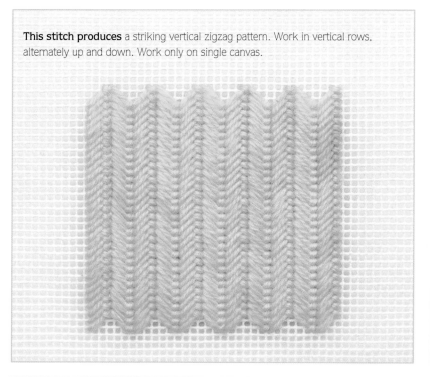

This stitch produces a striking vertical zigzag pattern. Work in vertical rows, alternately up and down. Work only on single canvas.

1 Work a diagonal stitch from lower left to upper right over 3 vertical and 3 horizontal rows, coming out 1 vertical thread to the left.

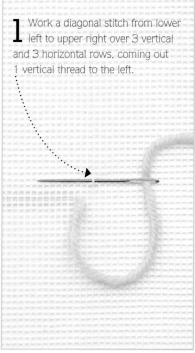

2 Cross this stitch with a stitch over 1 mesh, bringing the needle out 1 horizontal thread below starting point.

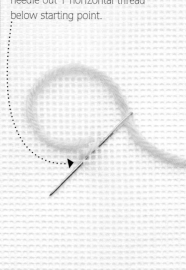

3 Repeat Step 1, coming up to the right of previously worked long stitch. Cross the long stitch with a short one, as in Step 2. Repeat Steps 1–2.

4 Work the next row upward (to right of the first). Come up 1 thread above the end of the last crossing stitch of the completed row and down 3 threads below and to right. Cross this with a stitch over 1 mesh.

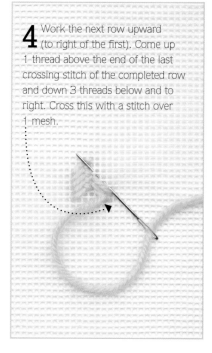

KNOTTED STITCH

Good for backgrounds, knotted stitch fills an area quickly and easily, producing an attractive braided effect.

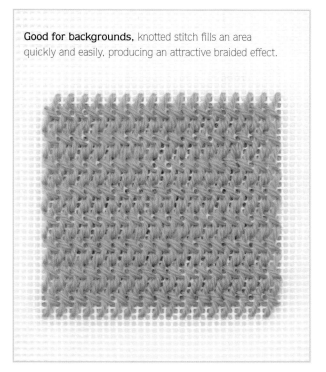

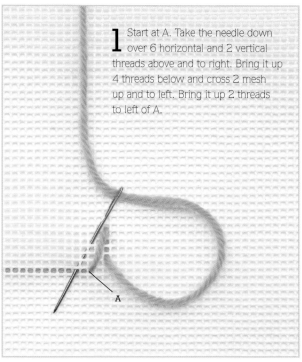

1 Start at A. Take the needle down over 6 horizontal and 2 vertical threads above and to right. Bring it up 4 threads below and cross 2 mesh up and to left. Bring it up 2 threads to left of A.

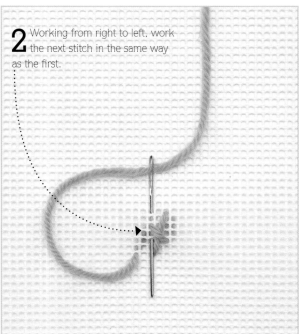

2 Working from right to left, work the next stitch in the same way as the first.

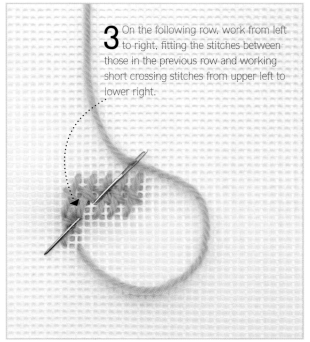

3 On the following row, work from left to right, fitting the stitches between those in the previous row and working short crossing stitches from upper left to lower right.

RICE STITCH

This popular stitch can also be worked in a single color.

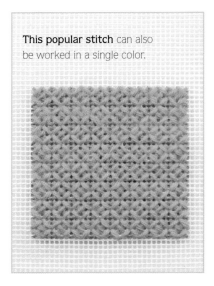

1 Work rows of cross stitches (see page 179), over 4 vertical and 4 horizontal threads.

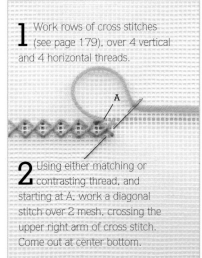

2 Using either matching or contrasting thread, and starting at A, work a diagonal stitch over 2 mesh, crossing the upper right arm of cross stitch. Come out at center bottom.

3 Cross the lower right arm with a second stitch, coming out center left to work the third stitch over the lower left arm. Come up at center top and work last stitch over upper left arm. Come out at center top of next stitch. Repeat.

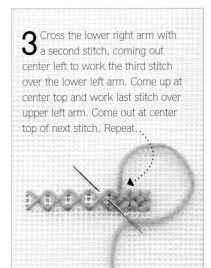

Loop Stitches

Some needlepoint stitches entail forming a loop of thread on the canvas. Here are two of the most useful. Pile stitch is worked on interlock or double canvas (including rug canvas), and preferably on a frame. These can be worked on double or single canvas.

CHAIN STITCH

This creates a flat texture resembling stockinette stitch in knitting and is useful for filling backgrounds. Work in vertical downward lines.

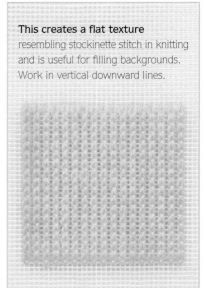

1 Come up at the top and take the needle down in the same hole, leaving a loop on the surface. Come up 2 canvas threads below the starting point, over the loop.

2 Pull the thread through (not too tightly) to form the first stitch.

3 At the end of the row, work a short stitch over 1 thread to secure the last loop. Leave 2 vertical threads between rows.

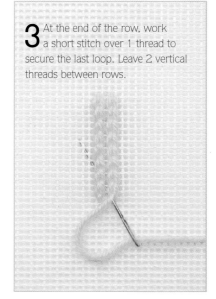

PILE STITCH

This produces a series of loops on the canvas, which can either be left uncut as shown or cut to produce a velvet effect.

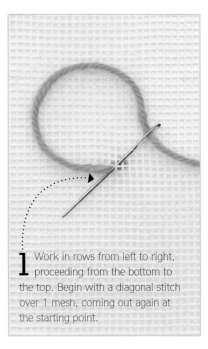

2 Take the needle down again over the same mesh. Come up 1 horizontal thread below, leaving a loop on the surface over the needle.

1 Work in rows from left to right, proceeding from the bottom to the top. Begin with a diagonal stitch over 1 mesh, coming out again at the starting point.

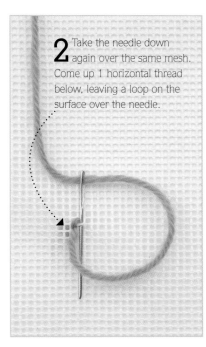

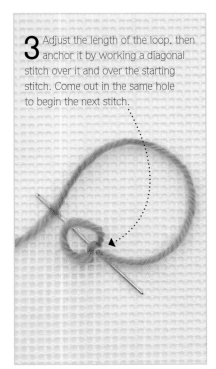

3 Adjust the length of the loop, then anchor it by working a diagonal stitch over it and over the starting stitch. Come out in the same hole to begin the next stitch.

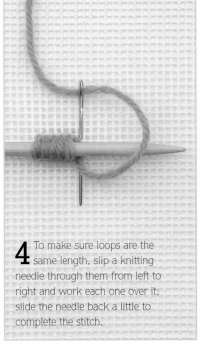

5 Work each following row over the canvas thread just above previously worked stitches. When all the stitches have been worked you can, if you wish, carefully cut through each row of loops using a small pair of scissors.

4 To make sure loops are the same length, slip a knitting needle through them from left to right and work each one over it; slide the needle back a little to complete the stitch.

Needlepoint designs **187**

Star stitches

The stitches in this section are formed of individual stitches radiating outward from one or more points, which may be in the center of the stitch or on one side of it. Unless otherwise stated, these stitches can be worked on either single or double canvas.

STAR STITCH

Also called Algerian eye, this simple but attractive stitch consists of eight stitches radiating from a central point. Use a relatively thick thread to cover the canvas. Work only on single canvas.

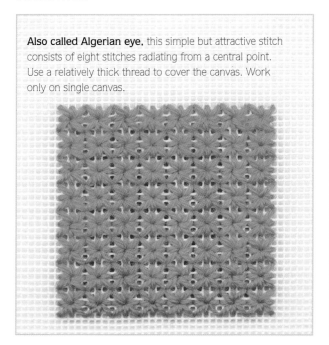

1 Work in horizontal rows, starting each stitch at the upper right-hand corner on right-to-left rows and the upper left-hand corner on left-to-right rows.

2 Come up at A and down over 2 mesh below left; this is the center. Work the next stitch over 2 horizontal threads, again into the center, and come up at the upper left-hand corner.

3 Continue to work counterclockwise around center. After working the eighth stitch, come up at the upper left-hand corner, ready to begin the next stitch.

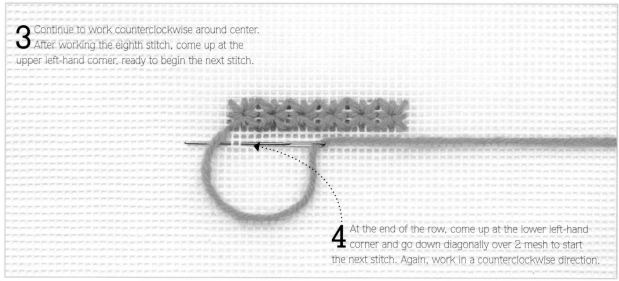

4 At the end of the row, come up at the lower left-hand corner and go down diagonally over 2 mesh to start the next stitch. Again, work in a counterclockwise direction.

FAN STITCH

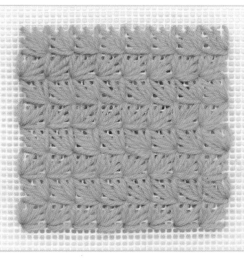

Also known as ray stitch, this is worked in alternate rows in different directions. For a denser version use nine stitches instead of five.

1 Start at A. Work a straight stitch over 4 horizontal threads. Work 4 more stitches radiating out from this corner point, to form a square over 4 horizontal/vertical threads. Note that there is a space (2 canvas threads) at the edge between each stitch; for a 9-stitch block, work into all the spaces.

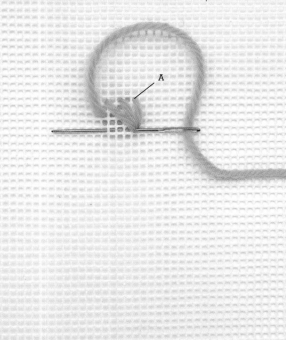

2 Work the next fan stitch immediately to the left, coming up at the top left-hand corner of the first stitch. Continue to the end of the row.

3 On the following row, work as before, but with the individual stitches pointing to the right.

DIAMOND EYELET STITCH

This decorative, large-scale stitch can be used either singly or as a background. Since 16 stitches must fit into the central hole, you can widen the hole with the points of embroidery scissors or use a relatively thin thread, such as soft embroidery floss. If you need to widen the holes to accommodate the thread, you should not use interlock or double canvas for this stitch.

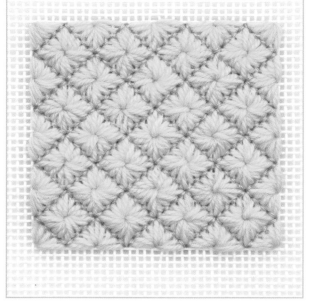

1 Bring the needle up at A, 4 threads left of center. Take down into center (B). Come up 3 vertical threads to left and 1 thread above. Take down at B. Come up under 2 vertical and 2 horizontal threads.

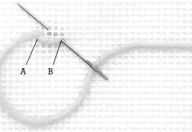

2 Continue working stitches around the center hole to form a diamond.

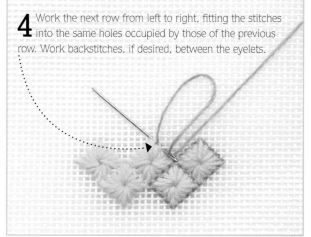

3 After working the 16th stitch, bring the needle up at A, where the first stitch emerged. Take it down 4 canvas threads to left; this will be the center hole for the next stitch. Work 16 stitches.

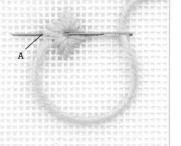

4 Work the next row from left to right, fitting the stitches into the same holes occupied by those of the previous row. Work backstitches, if desired, between the eyelets.

LEAF STITCH

This stitch is perfect for suggesting large-scale foliage. Use a smooth thread to show its structure to best advantage.

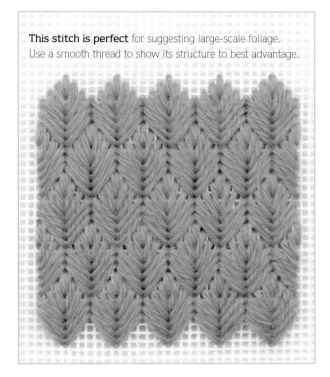

1 Work rows in alternate directions, from top to bottom. Beginning at the base of the leaf at A, work a diagonal stitch over 4 horizontal and 3 vertical threads to the left. Work 2 more identical stitches above.

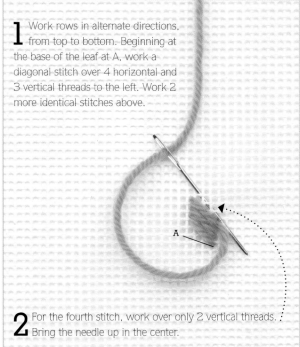

2 For the fourth stitch, work over only 2 vertical threads. Bring the needle up in the center.

3 For the fifth stitch, take the needle over 4 horizontal and 1 vertical thread. For the top stitch, skip 2 horizontal threads and work a stitch directly above the center line, over 3 threads.

4 Work the remaining 5 stitches as a mirror image of the first 5.

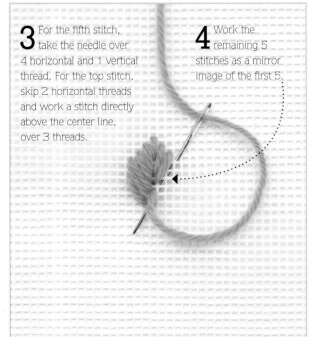

5 Begin the next stitch 6 vertical threads to the right (or left) of the base of the first one.

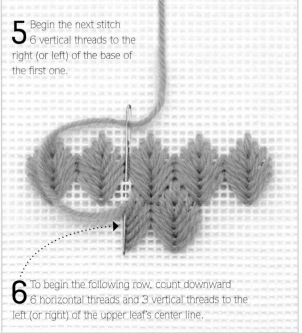

6 To begin the following row, count downward 6 horizontal threads and 3 vertical threads to the left (or right) of the upper leaf's center line.

Final touches

When you've worked the last stitch in your needlepoint, you now face the task of making it up into the finished article—a pillow cover or wall hanging, perhaps. The first step is to get the work itself into pristine condition.

Blocking and pressing

Blocking needlepoint gets the work back into shape if it has become distorted during stitching. Before you do this, hold the piece up to a strong light to check that no stitches are missing, and pull any wisps of yarn to the wrong side with the point of a tapestry needle.

WET BLOCKING

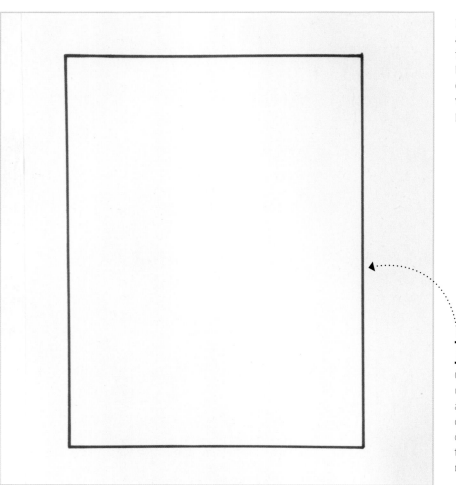

If the corners of your work are not square, you will need to wet-block it on a blocking board. This should be a piece of plywood or softwood that will accommodate fairly large pieces of work.

1 Measure 2 adjacent sides of the canvas. On a sheet of blotting paper, using a permanent marker and a set square and ruler, draw the correct outline of the canvas. Fasten the paper to the board at the corners with masking tape or thumbtacks.

2 Lay the needlepoint face down on the ironing board or on a clean thick towel and dampen it thoroughly with a wet sponge or a spray bottle.

3 Pull on the canvas in the direction opposite the distortion, starting at diagonally opposite corners and working toward the center.

4 Lay the wet needlepoint on the blocking board within the marked canvas outline (face down unless the work is highly textured). Secure it in place with thumbtacks, stretching the canvas to fit the outline.

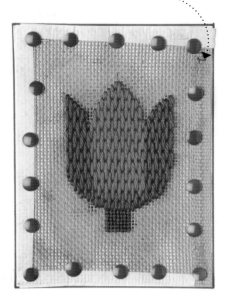

5 Leave the work to dry before removing it from the board. Check the corners of the needlepoint with the set square to make sure they are square.

DAMP PRESSING

In some cases, the needlepoint will fit the marked outline perfectly and can simply be damp-pressed. Place it face down on an ironing board (or face up if it is highly textured) and lay a damp cotton cloth on top. Gently place a hot, dry iron over the whole area, repeatedly setting the iron down and lifting it up—do not use an ironing motion. Leave the needlepoint to dry naturally before handling it.

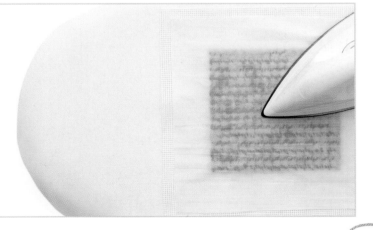

Seams and edges

Before joining a piece of needlepoint to a piece of fabric (as for a pillow cover), you should trim the edges to about ¾–1in (2–3cm); this will remove the selvage, if any, and any uneven edges of canvas caused in the blocking.

STITCHING SEAMS

If you are joining the work to fabric, use the zipper foot of the sewing machine, working on the needlepoint side and stitching as close to the needlepoint as possible. Use a heavy-duty needle (size 90 or 100) and strong thread. If you don't have access to a sewing machine, you will need to sew the seam by hand, using backstitch. Or take the work to a company that offers a finishing service.

REDUCING BULK

At the corners, trim the canvas (and other fabric layer, if any) diagonally across, as shown, leaving a scant ⅜in (1cm) between the stitched corner and the diagonally cut edge. Steam-press the seam open. Turn the work right side out, and gently but firmly push the corners out to a neat point.

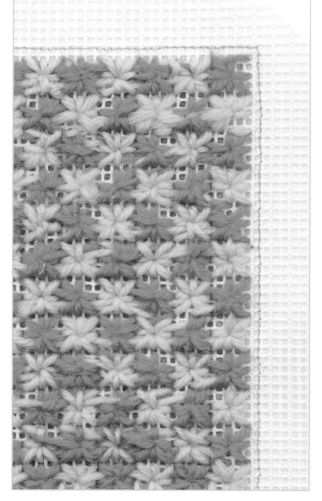

MITERING A CORNER

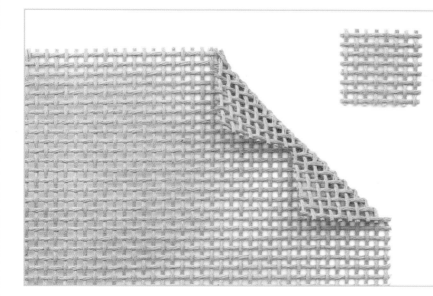

A piece that will be lined—for example, a wall hanging—will need to have the canvas edges turned to the wrong side. At the corners the canvas must be neatly mitered to produce as little bulk as possible. (Here, the miter is shown on bare canvas; in actuality, the needlepoint would extend to the fold).

1 Cut a small square out of the corner of the canvas, leaving 2 or 3 canvas threads at the inner corner. With the wrong side facing, fold the two canvas corners down to leave a diagonal fold.

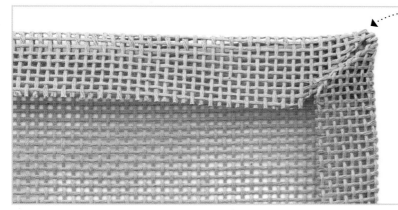

2 Fold the canvas edges to the wrong side, pressing them firmly with your fingers. Bring the folded edges over to meet diagonally, forming a miter, as shown.

3 Thread a chenille or large crewel needle with strong thread, such as button thread. Anchor this to the corner with a few backstitches, then oversew the mitered edges together firmly.

Lining a piece of needlepoint

You can line a piece of needlepoint by sewing it to the lining fabric right sides together, turning through a gap and slipstitching the opening closed. A neater result may be achieved by hand-stitching the lining in place. Use a firmly woven fabric for the lining.

1 Cut the lining the same size as the needlepoint, including seam allowances. Miter the corners of the needlepoint. Steam-press the canvas seam allowances down over the wrong side. (Here only canvas and lining are shown, to illustrate the principle).

2 Press the lining seam allowances to the wrong side and miter the corners.

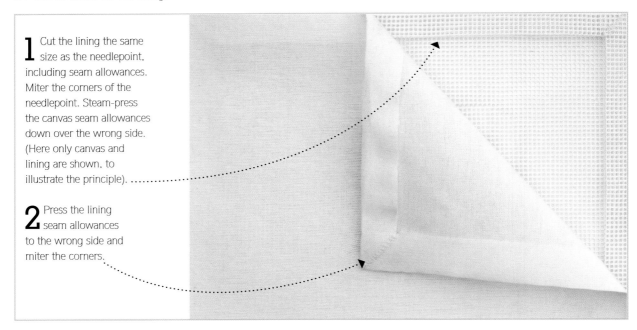

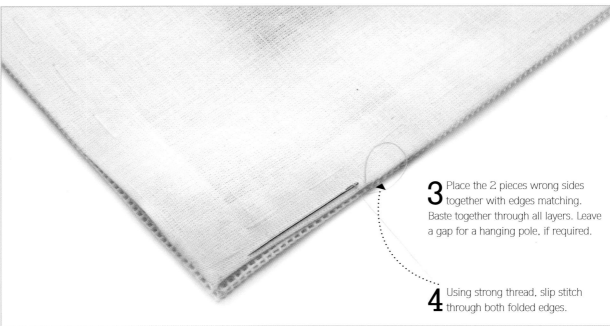

3 Place the 2 pieces wrong sides together with edges matching. Baste together through all layers. Leave a gap for a hanging pole, if required.

4 Using strong thread, slip stitch through both folded edges.

Lacing needlepoint over cardboard

If your project is a picture, intended for framing, you will need to lace it over a piece of cardboard. This method is also used for other embroidered pictures, but in the case of needlepoint, it is advisable to leave a small margin of bare canvas on the front, which can then be covered by the mount.

1 Cut a piece of cardboard the size of the needlepoint plus ¼in (5mm) all around. Remove the tape from the canvas edges, but leave a margin of canvas, 1½–2in (4–5cm) wide. Lay the canvas face down on a clean surface and place the cardboard on top.

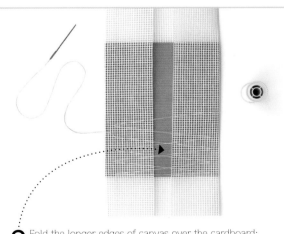

2 Fold the longer edges of canvas over the cardboard; hold them in place temporarily with pins stuck in the cardboard edges. Using a tapestry needle and strong thread attached to the spool, work herringbone stitches (see page 74) from one canvas edge to the other. Start at the center and work out to each side in turn.

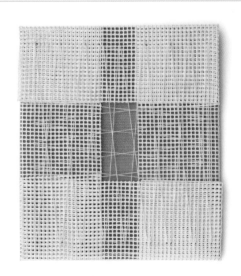

3 Repeat Step 2 to lace the 2 shorter sides together. Oversew the overlapping canvas edges at the corners.

Finishing and joining plastic canvas

One advantage of plastic canvas is that you don't need to worry about raw edges. You can finish or join plastic edges by oversewing with thread, using a tapestry needle.

FINISHING

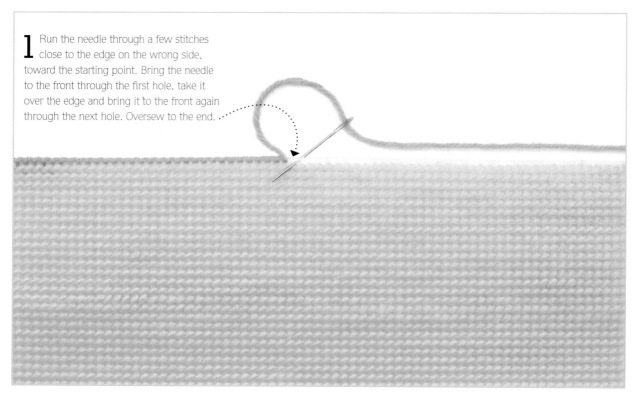

1 Run the needle through a few stitches close to the edge on the wrong side, toward the starting point. Bring the needle to the front through the first hole, take it over the edge and bring it to the front again through the next hole. Oversew to the end.

2 When you reach a corner, work 2 or 3 stitches into the same hole to cover the plastic edge completely.

3 Fasten off by taking the needle through a few stitches on the underside. Trim the end close to the stitches.

1 Fasten the thread on the wrong side of 1 piece
(see left). Place the 2 pieces together with wrong
sides facing and edges aligned.

2 Oversew through the corresponding holes. Pinch the edges together as you stitch so
that the stitches along the edge will lie smoothly.

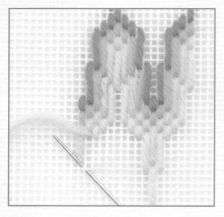
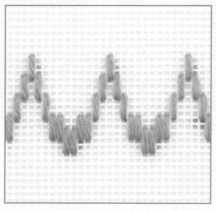
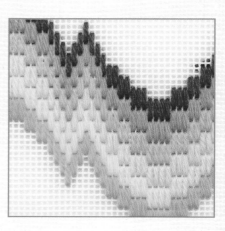

BARGELLO WORK

Bargello work

Also known as Florentine work, this distinctive style of needlepoint is named for the Italian city where it flourished in the sixteenth and seventeenth centuries. Its name of Bargello comes from the palace of that name in Florence. Today, Bargello work remains very popular, since it is so enjoyable to stitch.

Basic Bargello stitch

Use single canvas for Bargello work. A smooth effect is best achieved with several strands of crewel yarn, as shown in the samples that follow, although tapestry yarn (shown at bottom) and Persian yarn also work well.

This is simply straight gobelin stitch (see page 173) worked in a stepped pattern. Each stitch is the same length, and the stitches may be worked over 3, 4, or more threads.

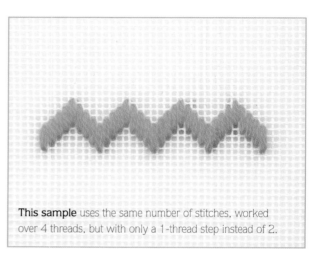

This sample uses the same number of stitches, worked over 4 threads, but with only a 1-thread step instead of 2.

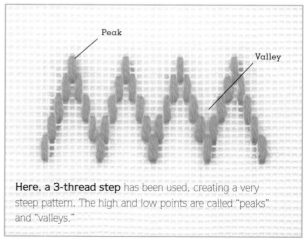

Peak

Valley

Here, a 3-thread step has been used, creating a very steep pattern. The high and low points are called "peaks" and "valleys."

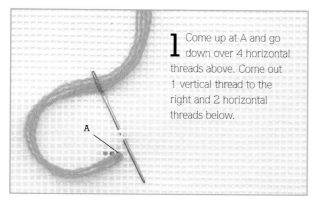

1 Come up at A and go down over 4 horizontal threads above. Come out 1 vertical thread to the right and 2 horizontal threads below.

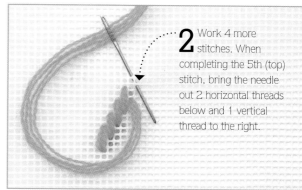

2 Work 4 more stitches. When completing the 5th (top) stitch, bring the needle out 2 horizontal threads below and 1 vertical thread to the right.

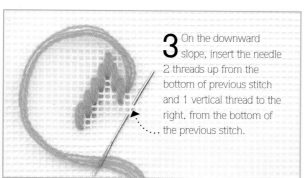

3 On the downward slope, insert the needle 2 threads up from the bottom of previous stitch and 1 vertical thread to the right, from the bottom of the previous stitch.

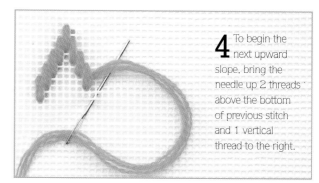

4 To begin the next upward slope, bring the needle up 2 threads above the bottom of previous stitch and 1 vertical thread to the right.

ALTERNATIVE METHOD

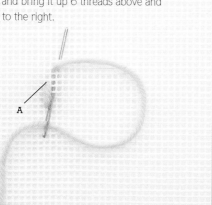

1 This produces longer stitches on the underside. Bring the needle out at the bottom of the "valley" at A. Take it down over 4 threads below, then bring it up 6 horizontal threads above and 1 vertical thread to right. Take it down 4 threads below and bring it up 6 threads above and 1 vertical thread to the right.

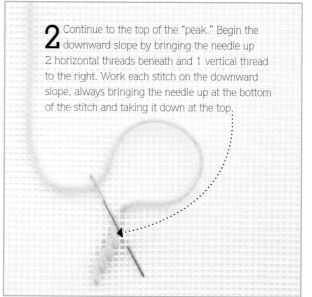

2 Continue to the top of the "peak." Begin the downward slope by bringing the needle up 2 horizontal threads beneath and 1 vertical thread to the right. Work each stitch on the downward slope, always bringing the needle up at the bottom of the stitch and taking it down at the top.

Variations on Bargello

A virtually infinite number of patterns can be created by varying the size and placement of the Bargello stitches. Here are just a few of them.

SWAGGED ZIGZAGS

Here the basic zigzag pattern has been widened and slightly curved by changing the bottom 2 stitches into 2-stitch blocks and working the top 3 stitches over 1-thread steps to form a steep pinnacle. All the stitches are the same size, covering 4 threads.

SCALLOPS

The use of wider blocks of stitches, along with a gradual variation in step depth, will produce curves. Here groups of 2, 3, and 5 stitches and a variation in step depth from 1 to 3 threads, have been used to produce scallops.

CURVES AND PINNACLES

Here the zigzag, shown left, has been lengthened by adding an extra 2-stitch block and turning the pinnacle upside down, forming an extended, sinuous line. Note that the lower part of the pattern is identical to the upper part.

CURVES AND PINNACLES (WIDENED)

Here the curves and pinnacles are given a shallower outline by working the stitches over 3 threads instead of 4.

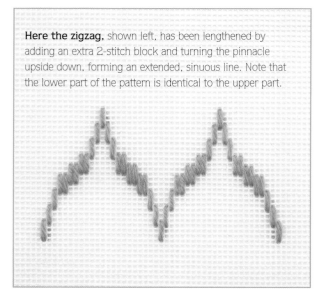

MOTIFS

Some Bargello patterns consist of motifs, rather than lines. These are produced by taking a section of a line pattern and working it as a mirror image. For example, the scallop row can be reversed to create an oval motif. Stitches within the motif can be shortened to meet in the middle.

SECONDARY MOTIFS

The spaces in between motifs are called secondary motifs. These can be worked in a modified or completely different color scheme. Here, a few stitches of black accentuate the space between motifs. You can also use a different stitch in this area, such as a single diamond eyelet (see page 190).

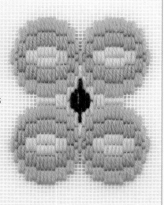

HUNGARIAN POINT

This variant of Bargello work has an ingenious pattern of long stitches combined with short ones. It is most effective worked in four closely related shades.

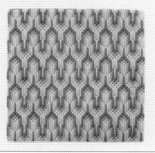

1 Work in rows from right to left. Establish the basic line, using the darkest color. Come up at A and down over 6 canvas threads below. Work a stitch over 2 threads, 1 vertical thread and 1 step down to the left. Repeat. Work 2 long stitches, each 1 step down from the previous stitch.

2 Work a stitch over 2 threads at the bottom, as shown. Repeat this sequence in reverse on the upward slope.

3 Work the next row directly under the first one, following a sequence of 2 short, 2 long, and 2 short. On the third row, work 1 short, 2 long, and 2 short, then work a long stitch at the bottom.

4 For the last row, work 2 long stitches, 2 short, and 2 long—the last stitch forming the lowest point of the pattern. Repeat these 4 rows to form the pattern.

Designing a Bargello project

If you'd like to try designing needlepoint but find the prospect a bit daunting, start with some Bargello designs. No drawing ability is required, and you don't have to hunt for source material. The simplest design technique is to take an existing pattern and change the colors, as shown below. You may wish first to consult a color wheel to familiarize yourself with the principles of color. Then buy some small skeins of your chosen colors and work a sample or two to see the effect.

CHANGE THE COLORS

This flame stitch pattern is worked in six colors. Here, the pink and green are contrasting, with the shape defined by the darker shades at top and bottom.

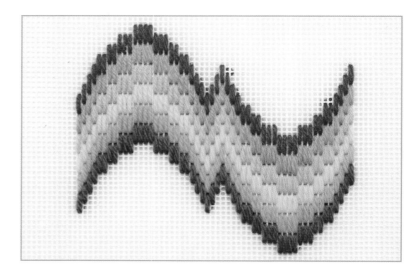

Here the cool green is contrasted with hot orange for an even more vibrant effect.

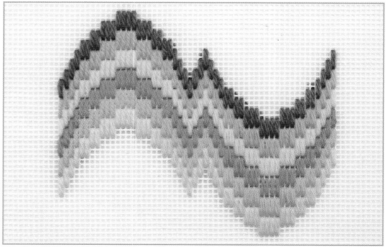

Hot colors can be combined successfully. Here pink and magenta are paired with warm yellows, with an intervening band of lilac to cool things down a little.

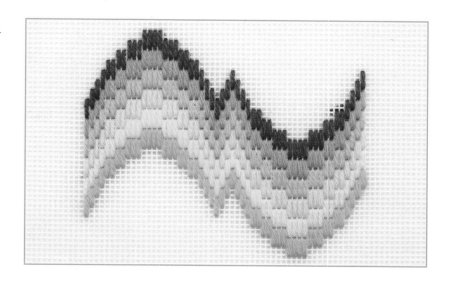

WORKING A BARGELLO PROJECT

It is important, when beginning a piece of Bargello work, to get the main line of the design correct, so take a little time over this. Mark the vertical center of your canvas; if the design is of the motif type (see page 205) you will also need to mark the horizontal center. Then find the center of the chart. Begin stitching at the center and work to one side; then work out to the other side. Check the stitches carefully against the chart. Once you are

sure that the pattern has been correctly established, you will find that (in most designs) the remaining rows will follow naturally. If the design is of the motif type (see, for example, the Pomegranate on page 210), you should begin by working the outline of the motif; then work the filling stitches. The same is true of the lattice-type design, such as the one shown on page 211.

Starting from scratch

To create your own Bargello design you will need some large-scale graph paper, a ruler, a pencil, some colored pencils, felt-tip pens, or crayons. A small rectangular mirror will also be useful.

PLANNING A ROW DESIGN

1 Begin by marking a random row of stitches across a piece of large-scale graph paper. Make sure they're all the same length and that any steps overlap the adjacent stitch by at least 1 grid (canvas) line.

2 Choose a section of the row that could make a pleasing design. If you have a mirror, move it along the row until you see a pattern that you like reflected symmetrically in it. Draw a line along the mirror, and draw another line to each side, equidistant from the center. This marks the repeat pattern.

3 Take another piece of graph paper large enough for your complete design, and mark the vertical center on it. Near the top of the paper, chart the stitches of the main row, starting at the center and working outward. Using colored pencils, pens, or crayons, add more rows below the main row; change the color scheme, if necessary. If you wish to design a motif-type Bargello pattern (see page 205), start with a row design, as in step 2, then run a mirror across the grid, at a 90-degree angle to the marked stitches until a pleasing motif emerges.

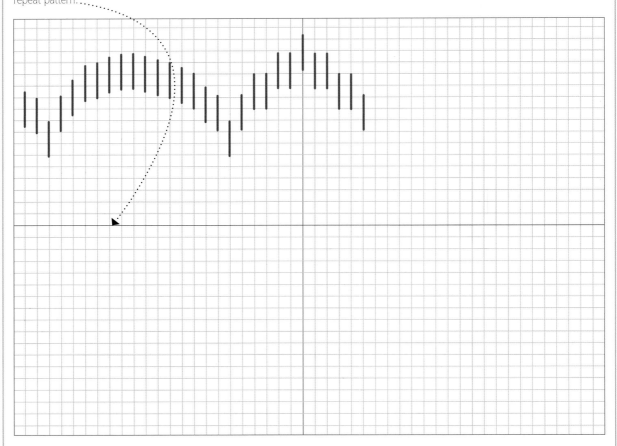

PLANNING A FOUR-WAY DESIGN

Also called kaleidoscope or mitered Bargello, these fascinating patterns consist of four identical quarters that meet in the center. Again, you should start with the dominant line of the pattern. You can begin at the outer edge of the design and work inward, or vice versa.

1 Using graph paper and a mirror, create a row pattern as described above. Draw a line through the center of the row, parallel to the stitch lines. Now place the mirror over the row at a 45-degree angle and move it along until a pleasing pattern appears. Draw a line diagonally to the center at this point.

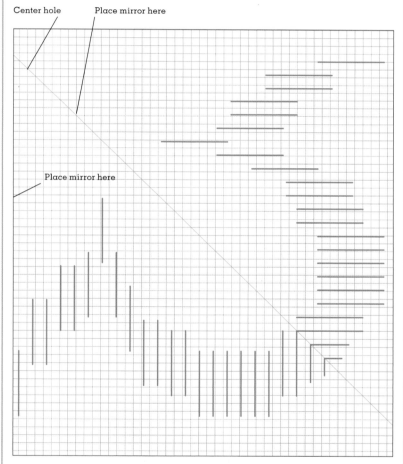

Center hole   Place mirror here

Place mirror here

2 Take another piece of graph paper, large enough for one-quarter of the whole design. Mark off a right angle in one corner. Mark a broken line through the grid at a 45-degree angle. Referring to the original, chart the stitches on the quarter of the design. Fill in the other colors. Aside from the dominant lines, these can be confined to one triangle.

TIPS FOR ADJUSTING

• **When charting** a symmetrical section of a row, check the position of two corresponding stitches by running a pencil lightly from the bottom of one stitch to the bottom of its "opposite number" to make sure they are aligned. Also check that you have the same number of stitches in both halves of the line or motif.

• **Some trial and error** is involved in designing Bargello work—especially the four-way designs. Once you've established your dominant line and transferred it to the full-size graph paper, make a few photocopies to use, if necessary, for color changes.

• **If you're not pleased** with the way a four-way pattern is developing along the diagonal, make a new chart, moving the dominant line inward or outward.

• **If the dominant line** will be interrupted at the edge of the design, you can either plan to make the needlepoint larger or smaller or choose a different-gauge canvas.

Bargello designs

Here are five Bargello designs, which you can work as shown or vary as you please, changing the colors or the patterns themselves, as described on pages 204–205.

POMEGRANATE

The Pomegranate motif is a Bargello classic. When the motifs are placed together a fascinating 3-D effect is produced. You could, instead, work a single line of joined motifs on a background of shaded rows of straight gobelin stitch (see page 173). Each stitch goes over 4 canvas threads.

UNDULATING STRIPES

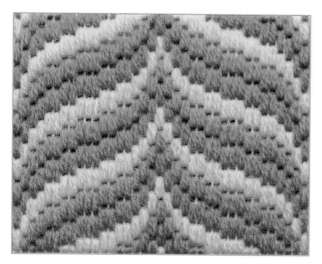

These undulating stripes have a restful rhythm. To accentuate the horizontal character just three colors are used, but you could add more colors for more vertical interest. Each stitch goes over 3 canvas threads.

FLAMES

This is a typical "flame stitch" Bargello pattern, using six colors; you can use more or fewer if you prefer. Each stitch in this version goes over 6 canvas threads.

Ws

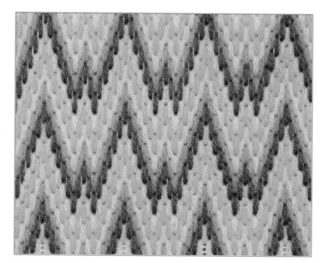

Another traditional Bargello pattern, "Ws" produces a jagged, spiky effect. Here five colors are used, and each stitch goes over 4 canvas threads.

LATTICE

This fascinating lattice design requires a bit of study to get right, but is well worth the effort. There are 7 long (6-thread) stitches in each strip of the lattice, and each strip finishes with a 4-thread and a 2-thread stitch at each end. If you like, you could use two shades of one color for the lattice and two colors in the central spaces.

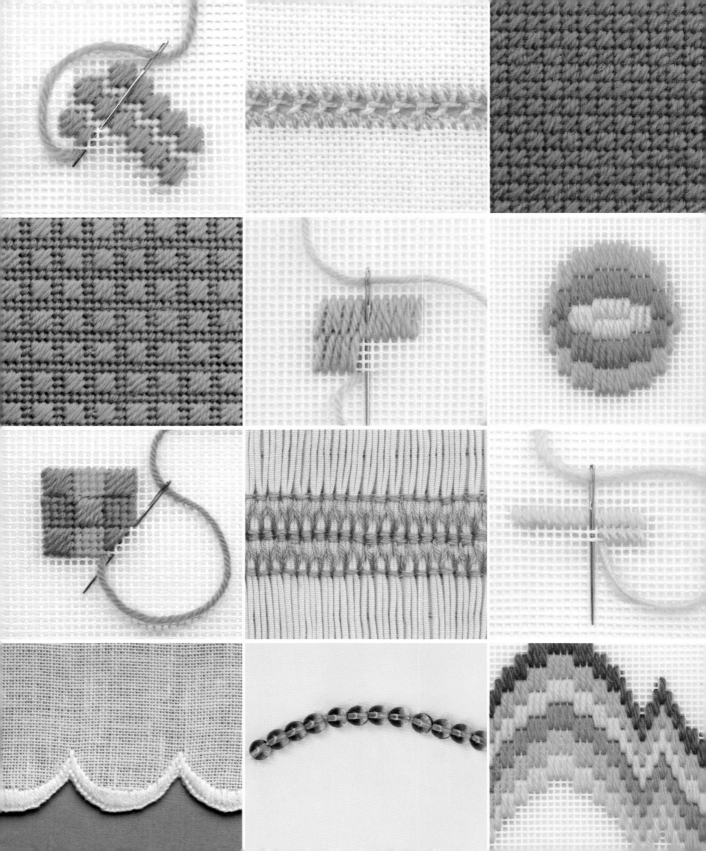

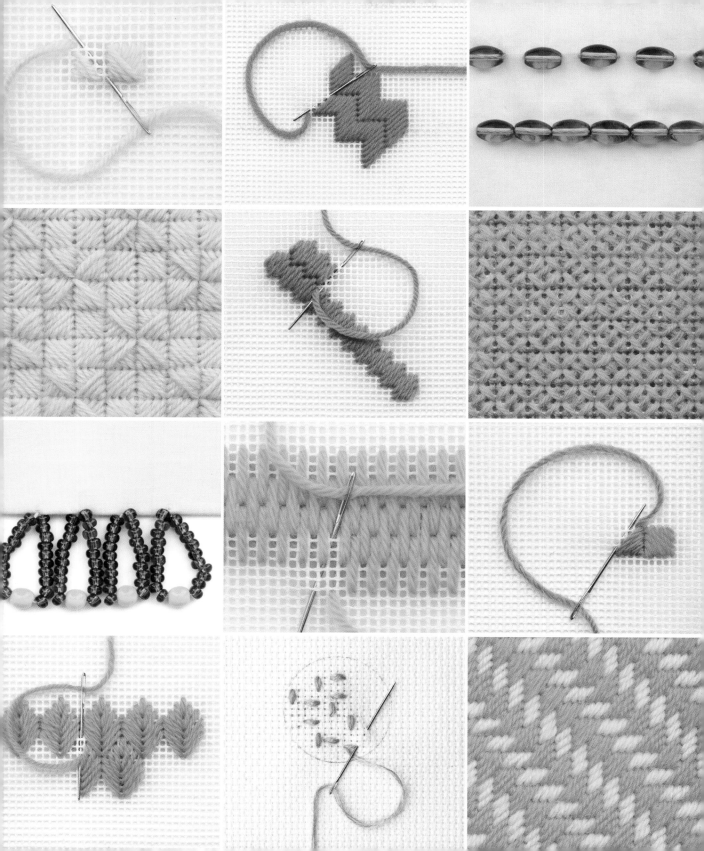

Glossary

Bargello work
A style of needlepoint that developed in Florence, Italy, in the sixteenth and seventeenth centuries and is characterized by stepped stitches that create curved or zigzag patterns; also known as Florentine work.

Bias
The diagonal grain of a woven fabric, at 45 degrees to the straight grain.

Binding
A narrow strip of fabric used to cover the raw edges of a piece of embroidery to provide a neat finish and prevent it from fraying. For straight edges, the binding can be cut on the straight grain; bias-cut binding has more stretch, and should always be used for curved edges.

Blocking
In needlepoint, manipulating a finished piece into the correct shape by wetting and pinning it out, or pinning it out and steam pressing it.

Broderie anglaise
A type of openwork embroidery in which the design consists mainly of small holes edged with buttonhole stitch; also known as eyelet lace. Broderie anglaise is traditionally worked in white thread on white fabric.

Couching
An embroidery technique in which a thread is laid over the surface of the fabric and attached by means of tiny "tying" stitches worked vertically or diagonally across it.

Count
The number of threads or holes per 1in (2.5cm) in each direction of an even-weave fabric or needlepoint canvas; the more threads, the finer the fabric.

Crossways grain
See Weft.

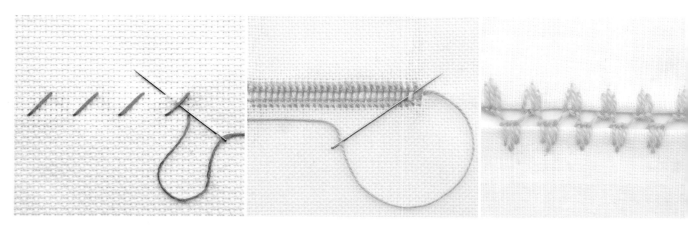

Cutwork

A type of openwork embroidery in which areas of the fabric are stitched and the background fabric is then cut away to form lacy patterns. Like broderie anglaise, it is traditionally worked in white thread on white fabric.

Drawn thread work

An openwork embroidery technique that involves pulling individual threads from an even-weave fabric, leaving a "ladder" of threads in one direction, or an area that can be worked by stitching over groups of threads in a regular pattern.

Even-weave fabric

A fabric that has the same number of threads running from left to right as from top to bottom. It is used for counted-thread techniques such as cross stitch and needlepoint. Examples of even-weave fabrics include even-weave linen, Aida cloth, Binca, and Hardanger.

Faggoting

See Insertions.

Florentine work

See Bargello work.

Insertions

Decorative embroidery stitches worked over an open space between two pieces of fabric to join them together; also known as "faggoting."

Lengthwise grain

See Warp.

Mirrorwork

Also called shisha work, a traditional form of textile decoration from Central Asia and India that involves stitching around or over small disks of mirror, glass, or tin to hold them in place on the fabric.

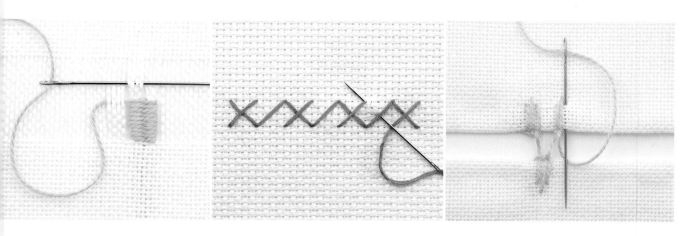

Miter

To finish a corner by stitching adjacent sides of fabric together at a 45-degree angle.

Openwork embroidery

An overall term for a number of embroidery techniques that open up areas of the background fabric to create lacelike effects. *See also* broderie anglaise, cutwork, drawn thread work, insertions, pulled thread work, whitework.

Plain-weave fabric

A tightly woven fabric in which the warp and weft form a simple crisscross pattern. The number of threads in each direction is not necessarily equal. Examples of plain-weave fabrics include cotton, linen, and silk.

Pulled thread work

An openwork embroidery technique in which threads on an even-weave fabric are pulled together with tight stitches to create regular spaces.

Right side

The front of a piece of fabric; the side that will normally be in view when the piece is made up.

Seam

The join formed when two pieces of fabric are sewn together.

Selvage

The rigid edge woven into each side of a length of fabric to prevent the fabric from fraying or unraveling. It occurs when the weft thread turns at the edge of the warp threads to start the next row.

Shisha

See **Mirrorwork.**

Smocking

A form of embroidery that involves gathering fabric into tight folds and then working decorative stitches over the gathers. Traditionally used to decorate the gathers in

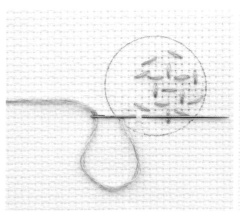  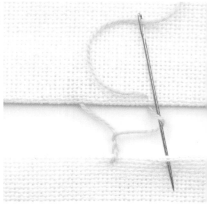

the bodices of dresses, blouses, baptismal gowns, and smocks.

Straight grain
The threads of a woven fabric running parallel to, or at 90 degrees to, either the lengthwise (warp) or crosswise (weft) direction of the weave.

Surface embroidery
The general term for decorative surface stitchery usually worked on plain-weave fabric. Most techniques on even-weave fabric are openwork.

Tension
The relative tightness used by the stitcher in needlepoint and pulled thread work.

Tramé, tramming
In needlepoint, the technique of laying long horizontal stitches to provide a foundation for other stitches.

Warp
The vertical threads of a woven fabric, also known as the lengthwise grain.

Weft
The horizontal threads of a woven fabric, also known as the crosswise grain.

Whitework
A generic term for the embroidery techniques of cutwork and broderie anglaise, which are traditionally worked in white thread on delicate white plain-weave fabrics such as lawn, fine linen, cambric, and voile.

Wrong side
The reverse of a piece of fabric; the side that will normally be hidden from view when the piece is made up.

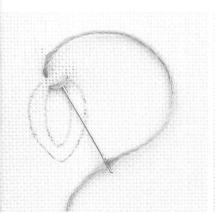
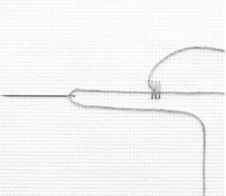

Index

About the authors

Maggi Gordon, author of the embroidery chapters, is a freelance editor and author specializing in craft, home, and lifestyle. She lives in Wisconsin and is the author of 14 needlecraft books, including *The Ultimate Quilting Book* (1999), *The Ultimate Sewing Book* (2002), *The Complete Book of Quilting* (2005), and *The Needlecraft Book* (2010).

Ellie Vance, author of the needlepoint chapters, is a writer and freelance editor specializing in needlecrafts. She has designed and made original embroidery, needlepoint, and patchwork projects for various books and magazines. Born in the United States, she now makes her home in England.

Authors' acknowledgments

Maggi Gordon: Thanks to everyone at Dorling Kindersley who contributed to this book, especially Mary-Clare Jerram, who commissioned me, and Danielle Di Michiel, the most patient of editors, and to Heather, who was my original point of contact. And as always to David, whose support has been unwavering.

Ellie Vance: I would like to express my thanks to Katie Hardwicke, for her sensitive editing and fine attention to detail, and to the team at Dorling Kindersley for all their hard work, especially to Danielle Di Michiel, for her outstanding efficiency and unfailing good humor.

Publisher's acknowledgments

Heema Sabharwal for design; Hilary Bird for indexing; Willow Fabrics and House of Smocking for materials and equipment; Usha International for sewing machines.

Creative technicians:
Arijit Ganguly, Archana Singh, Amini Hazarika, Bani Ahuja, Chanda Arora, Christelle Weinsberg, Eleanor Van Zandt, Evelin Kasikov, Geeta Sikand, Indira Sikand, Kusum Sharma, Medha Kshirsagar, Meenal Gupta, Nandita Talukder, Nalini Barua, Neerja Rawat, Resham Bhattacharjee, Suchismita Banerjee. Special thanks to Bishnu Sahoo, Vijay Kumar, Rajesh Gulati, Tarun Sharma, Sanjay Sharma.

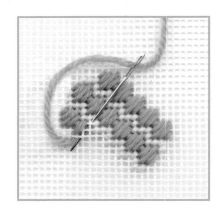